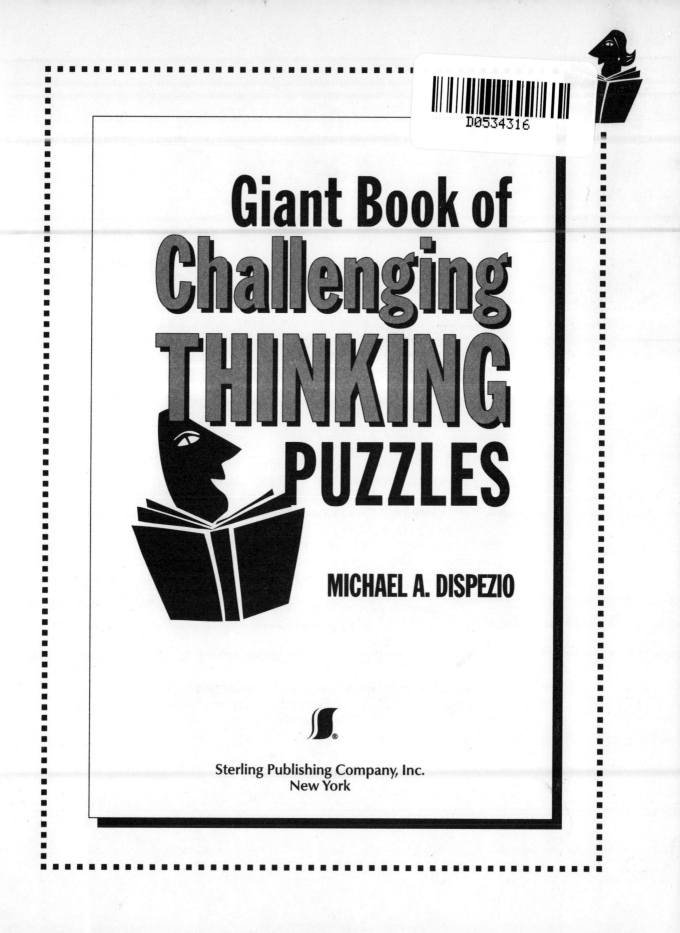

Giant Book of
Challenging
THINKING
PUZZLES

MICHAEL A. DISPEZIO

Sterling Publishing Company, Inc.
New York

Material in this collection was adapted from:

Critical Thinking Puzzles,
Great Critical Thinking Puzzles,
Challenging Critical Thinking Puzzles, and
Visual Thinking Puzzles
© Michael A. DiSpezio

4 6 8 10 9 7 5

Published by Sterling Publishing Co., Inc.
387 Park Avenue South, New York, NY 10016
© 2003 by Sterling Publishing Co., Inc.
Distributed in Canada by Sterling Publishing
℅ Canadian Manda Group, 165 Dufferin Street
Toronto, Ontario, Canada M6K 3H6
Distributed in Great Britain by Chrysalis Books Group PLC
The Chrysalis Building, Bramley Road, London W10 6SP, England
Distributed in Australia by Capricorn Link (Australia) Pty. Ltd.
P.O. Box 704, Windsor, NSW 2756, Australia

Sterling ISBN 1-4027-1090-9

For information about custom editions, special sales, premium and
corporate purchases, please contact Sterling Special Sales
Department at 800-805-5489 or specialsales@sterlingpub.com

CONTENTS

SECTION 1

SECTION 2

SECTION 3

SECTION 4

Section 1
Critical Thinking
PUZZLES

Introduction

When we think critically we are engaging in intellectual strategies to probe the basic nature of a problem, situation, or puzzle. By these strategies, we mean making observations, predictions, generalizations, reasonings by assumptions, comparisons and contrasts, uncovering relationships between the parts to the whole, and looking for sequences. It sounds like a lot, but everyone has these skills and the puzzles in this book are designed to challenge, exercise, and stretch the way you interpret the world.

Some of the puzzles here are old favorites that have entertained people for years. Several of them are presented in their time-tested way. Most of the standards, however, have a new twist or updated story added. Other puzzles require some inventive solutions, so don't be afraid to be creative. Most of them can be done with a pencil or pen.

Some require inexpensive materials that can probably be found around the house: a pair of scissors, markers, tape, toothpicks, and a yardstick. Even though some puzzles can be solved using algebra, they were selected for their ability to be visualized and figured out this way. Therefore, in addition to being fun to do, they offer an arena to practice thinking skills.

Statements such as "I want you to memorize this list" or "That's a good answer, but it wasn't the one I expected" help to extinguish critical thought. Although you'll never have to measure an ant's path or alter a flag, the process of creating and evaluating a reasonable answer is a worthwhile experience. By the time you finish this section, those powerful skills will be back on track, probing your everyday experiences for a more thorough and deeper understanding.

Ready to start? Great, because the fun is about to begin.

—Michael

Pyramid Passage

Ancient Egyptian pyramids were built as royal tombs. Within these massive stone structures were rooms, halls and connecting passageways. Look at the figure below. Can you draw four paths that connect the matching symbols? The paths may not cross, they may not enter a non-matching pyramid, nor may they go outside the large pyramid boundary.

Magic Pyramid

For this pyramid, can you place the numbers 1,2,3,4,5, and 6 in the circles shown below? Only one number may be placed in a circle and all numbers must be used. When the final arrangement is complete, the sum of each side's three numbers must all be the same number.

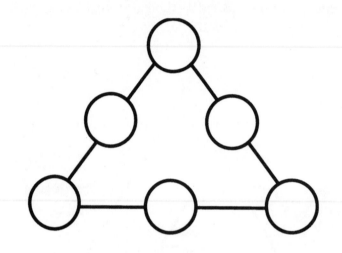

Pyramid Builders

The Egyptian pyramids at Giza are incredible structures that took many years to complete. They were constructed out of large rectangular stone blocks, each weighing about as much as a car. The two largest pyramids contain over two million of these blocks!

Now, it's your turn to work. Can you build a three dimensional pyramid using two odd-shaped blocks?

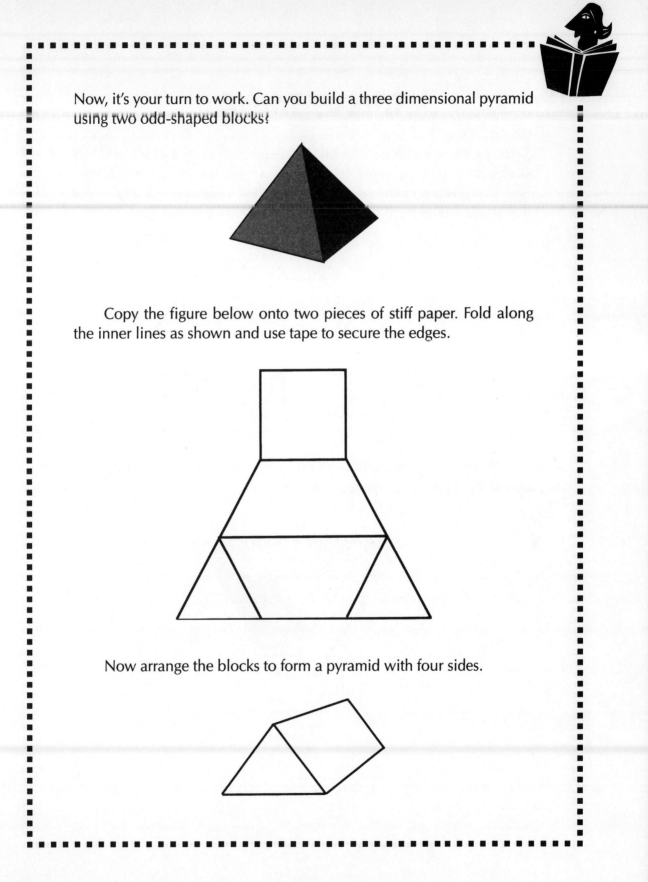

Copy the figure below onto two pieces of stiff paper. Fold along the inner lines as shown and use tape to secure the edges.

Now arrange the blocks to form a pyramid with four sides.

9

Trial by Triangle

Take a look at these two identical triangles. They are made with six sticks.

Can you rearrange the sticks so that they form four triangles? All of the new triangles must be the same size as these original two!

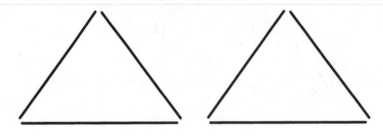

By the way, here's a triangle that you can draw but can't build. It's called an impossible triangle. See why?

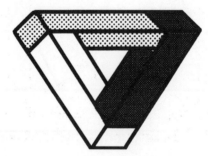

Before you go on to the next puzzle, take a look at these strange objects. Do you think that they can also be built? Or do you think there may be some sort of trick?

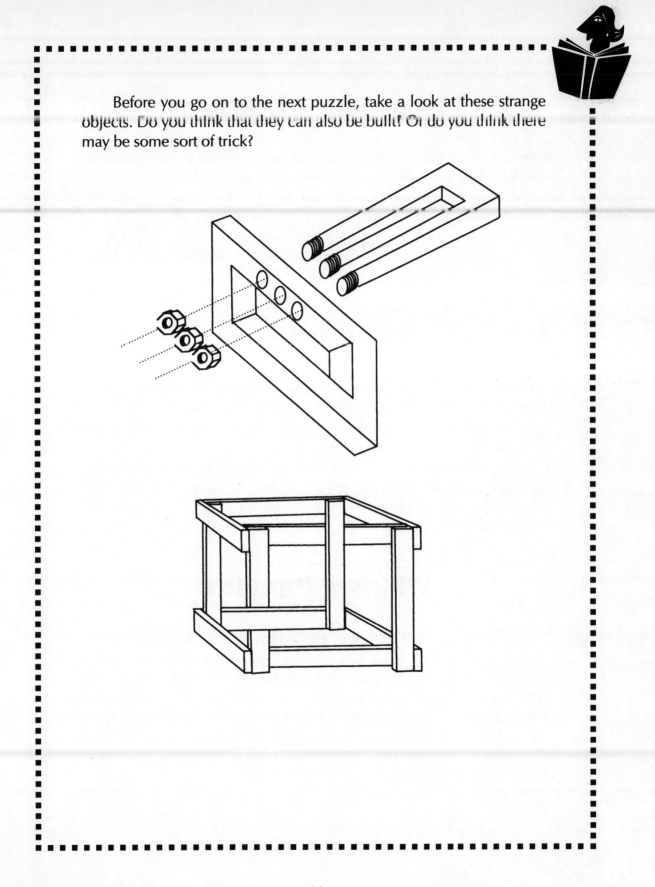

Trapezoid 2 Triangle

Here's another triangle whose only problem is that it isn't built yet. You'll have to assemble it from these three trapezoids!

Spare My Brain

To move their armies, the Romans built over 50,000 miles of roads. Imagine driving all those miles! Now imagine driving those miles in the first gasoline-driven car that has only three wheels and could reach a top speed of about 10 miles per hour.

For safety's sake, let's bring along a spare tire. As you drive the 50,000 miles, you rotate the spare with the other tires so that all four tires get the same amount of wear. Can you figure out how many miles of wear each tire accumulates?

Whirling Paradox

Let's take a closer look at those tires. If a car with spoke wheels drives by, we will see that when the spinning spokes get to the top of the wheel, they are moving so fast that they become blurred. At the same time, the spokes on the bottom half of the wheel appear to be moving much slower. In fact, they are so slow that you may be able to count them. If the spokes are connected to the same wheel, how can this be?

HINT: There may be a connection between this observation and the sound of a speeding car as it zooms by.

Lost?

Now we're on foot. Imagine that you and several friends have hiked into a remote region of the countryside. Your final destination is the land of Ultima. After leaving the village of Skullara, you continue following the trail and come across an important intersection. There is, however, one slight problem.

The sign showing which way to go has been knocked down. How can you figure out what is the right direction you need to go?

Sand Traps

As you continue on your hike, you're handed a map of the terrain ahead. This is not a safe place. In fact, the entire region is filled with quicksand, which is shown on the map as black splotches. Contrary to belief, quicksand does not suck or pull you under. Instead, it's your weight that makes you sink in this water and fine sand mixture.

Your challenge is to discover a path from any point on the bottom edge of the map to any point on the top edge without running into quicksand (black splotches). To make it more challenging, the path must consist of only two straight lines.

To start, place your pencil anywhere on the bottom border of the map. Then draw a straight line. When you stop, don't lift the pencil. Complete your trip using one more straight line.

Which Mountain?

Now that you've made it past the quicksand, it's time to do some climbing. You have a choice of climbing one of three geometrically shaped mountains, which are all 10,000 feet high. One of the mountains is a perfect cylinder, another is in the shape of a cone, and the third looks like the top half of a sphere. Several out-of-work math teachers have constructed roads that go from the base to the summit of each mountain. All three roads are built so that you climb 1 vertical foot every 20 horizontal feet. If you wish to walk the shortest distance from base to summit, which mountain would you choose?

Compass Caper

A compass is a reliable tool that always point north—or does it? There are many reports of compass needles that unexpectedly turn away from north. The strangest natural cause for this disturbance may be a shooting star. As the meteor streaks across the sky, it upsets the electrical balance of the air and produces a magnetic force that some believe affects the compass reading.

We, however, will work with a compass that always gives a true heading. Suppose you start a hike by traveling directly south for 500 paces. Then, you turn and go due east for another 100 paces. You turn once more and go due north for 500 paces. You are now in the exact same spot where you started from, but in front of you is a bear. What color is it?

A Cut Above

With all that hiking, you've probably now worked up an appetite. So how about some pizza?

Suppose this is the early 1900's and you're in New York City's Little Italy getting a Pizza Margherita, named in honor of a pizza-loving Italian princess. Can you divide the pie into eight equal slices in only three straight cuts? All the pieces must be identical: each with an upper surface covered with sauce, lower baked crust, and a crusty edge.

HINT: Don't worry about the mess. You won't have to clean it.

Kitchen Cups

Have you ever seen the written form of the Sanskrit language? If so, you probably are amazed at how different this ancient language from India looks from ours. Some English words, however, are based on Sanskrit. For example, cup comes from the Sanskrit word *kupa*, which means water well. This puzzle requires several water wells.

Suppose you need to measure exactly 1 cup of water. All that you have in your kitchen are two containers. The smaller container holds 3 cups and the larger holds 5 cups. How can you use these two containers to measure exactly 1 cup of water?

Moldy Math

Now let's talk about something else that you might have, but not want, in your kitchen. While you are raiding the refrigerator, you look behind the stove and discover a slice of bread that you misplaced several weeks ago. Needless to say, it is covered with mold. Since the mold started growing, the area it has covered has doubled each day. By the end of the eighth day, the entire surface of the bread is covered. When was the bread half-covered with mold?

And a Cut Below

Have you ever heard of the cheesemobile? It's a giant refrigerated truck that was built to carry a piece of Cheddar cheese. Why, then, all the fuss? Simple. The cheese weighed over 40,000 pounds!

Take a look a the smaller barrel of cheese below. If you make these three complete and straight cuts, how many pieces of cheese will you have?

Egg Exactly

Suppose you have only two egg timers, a 5-minute and a 3-minute. Can you use these two measuring devices to time an egg that must be boiled for exactly 2 minutes?

WHY AGAIN DID YOU SAY YOU WANTED TO KNOW THIS?

Losing Marbles?

Marbles have been around for a long time. In fact, archaeologists have discovered marbles buried alongside an Egyptian child who died over 4000 years ago! The word "marble," however, comes from the Greek word *marmaros*, which is a white polished stone made from the mineral agate.

Now it's your turn to play with them. Place a marble in a cup and carry it to the opposite side of the room. Too easy, huh! To make this more challenging, the cup must be turned upside down. This may take a little bit of creative problem solving, but it can be done.

A Puzzle of Portions

Did you know that 3 ounces plus 3 ounces doesn't always equal 6 ounces? As illogical as this may sound, its true because of the behavior of the small particles (and spaces) that make up liquids. When different liquids are mixed, the particles tend to fill in some of the open spaces. As a result, the liquid becomes more compact and occupies less volume. It's only a small difference, but it is measurable.

Let's try mixing something whose volume does not change. Your challenge is to split some apple juice into three equal portions. The juice comes in a 24-ounce container. You have only three other containers, each holding 5, 11, and 13 ounces. How can you divide the juice into three equal portions?

HINT: At the very least, it will take four steps.

Mixed Up?

Root beer, not cola, is the oldest-marketed soft drink in America. Before it was sold in the United States, root beer was brewed in many colonial homes. It contained many ingredients including molasses, licorice, vanilla, and the bark from birch trees. It was going to be called root tea but was later changed to root beer to attract the tavern crowd.

Here is one 8-ounce cup filled with root beer and another 8-ounce cup filled with cola. Take 1 tablespoon of root beer and add it to the cola. Stir the mixture. Now take 1 tablespoon of the mixture and add it to the root beer. Is there more root beer in the cola or cola in the root beer?

Toothpick Teasers

For the puzzles in this group, you can also use pieces of straws or small sticks if you don't have toothpicks.

These six toothpicks are arranged in a hexagon. Starting with this arrangement, can you form two identical diamonds by moving only two toothpicks and adding just one more?

These sixteen toothpicks form eight identical triangles. Can you remove four toothpicks so that four of these triangles are left? All of the toothpicks that remain must be a side of the triangles with no loose ends sticking out.

Form four (and only four) identical squares by removing eight toothpicks.

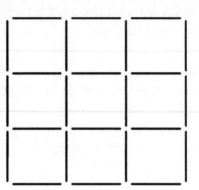

Move only three of the toothpicks (and the eye) to make the fish swim in the opposite direction.

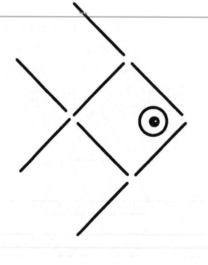

Going to the Movies

Let's take a break from these puzzles and go to the movies. The map below shows an assortment of routes from your home (H) to the movie theater (M). If you can only travel in a north, east, or northeast direction, how many possible routes are there from your home to the theater?

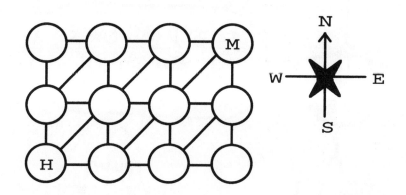

Now Seating?

Suppose two boys and three girls go to the movie theater and they all sit in the same row. If the row has only 5 seats:

1. How many different ways can the two boys and three girls be seated in this row?
2. What are the chances that the two children at the ends of the row are both boys?
3. What are the chances that the two children at the ends of the row are both girls?

Weighing In...

The movie playing in the theater is about a scientist who changes into a fly. Before she transforms herself, she carefully weighs a jar of sleeping flies. Then, she shakes the jar to wake them up. While they are flying, the scientist weighs the jar again. Does the jar full of flies weigh less when the insects are flying?

The Strangest Eyes

The scientist has transformed herself into a fly. One of her eyes is made up of one loop coiled into a spiral-like design. The other eye is made up of two separate loops shaped into a similar design. Can you tell which eye is the single loop and which one is the double without tracing the lines with a pencil?

Monkey Business

The theater shows a double feature. The second movie is about Tarzan going into the moving business.

For his first job, Tarzan must raise a 35-pound crate into his neighbor's tree house. To do this, he first attaches a pulley to a tree branch. He then passes a rope through the pulley and ties it to the crate. Just as he is about to lift the crate, he is called away to help a nearby elephant.

A passing chimp observes the situation and decides to help. The chimp also weighs 35 pounds. As the chimp pulls down on the rope what happens to the crate?

Head Count

In the final scene, a pet store owner is counting the birds and lizards that Tarzan has delivered to her store. For some odd reason, she decides to tally only the heads and scaly legs of these animals. When she has finished, she has counted thirty heads and seventy legs. How many birds and how many lizards are there?

Möbius Strip

Here is one of the strangest loops you'll ever see. It's called a Möbius strip in honor of the German mathematician who first investigated its properties.

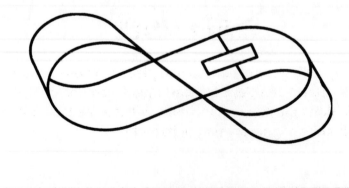

To build a Möbius strip, you need a strip of paper about 1 inch wide and 10 inches long. Coil the paper into a simple loop. Then put a single twist in the loop before securing the ends together with a piece of tape. Use a marker to color one side of the strip red and the other side blue. You'll soon discover that this loop has only one side!

Möbius strips are used in manufacturing. Many machines have belts that are used to connect different spinning parts. By using a belt sewn into a Möbius strip, the belt wears evenly on both sides.

Suppose you divide right down the middle of the Möbius strip. What shape would you get? Make a guess; then use a pair of scissors to carefully divide the strip.

Aunt Möbius?

THINK ABOUT IT! If we place two ants side by side on a Möbius strip and start them off in opposite directions, they will first pass each other on opposite sides of the paper. Then one ant will be walking on the top side of the strip, while the other will be on the bottom side!

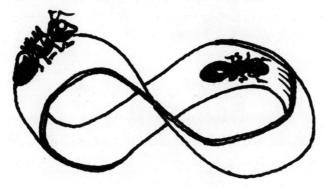

Ant Walk

Let's pick up an ant from the strip and place it on one corner of a sugar cube. This cube has sides all measuring 1 centimeter. If the ant can only walk along the edges of the cube, what is the total distance it can travel without retracing any part of its path?

Cubic Quandaries

A wooden cube is painted red. Suppose it is divided with six equal cuts into the smaller cubes as shown.

1. How many smaller cubes are there?
2. How many of these smaller cubes
    a. have only one side that is painted red?
    b. have two sides that are painted red?
    c. have three sides that are painted red?
    d. have no sides that are red?

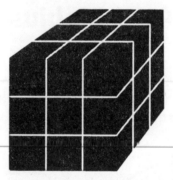

Squaring Off

Make a copy of these four rectangles. Cut out the shapes and then arrange them to form a perfect square.

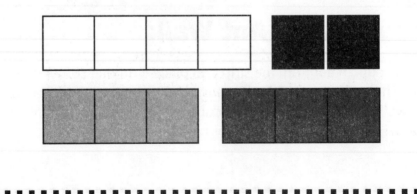

Saving Face

How good are you at visualizing things? These next few puzzles test your ability to rotate and construct objects in your mind.

These blocks below represent the same block. What figure is missing on the upper face of the last block?

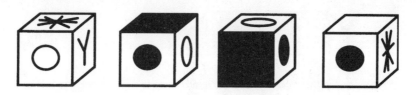

Which of the four cubes below can be created by folding this design?

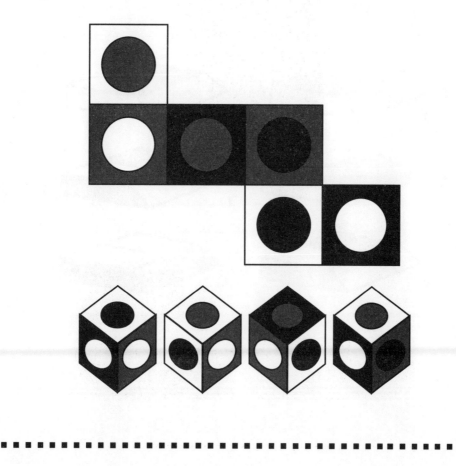

Finally, if you fold up this flat sheet along the inner lines, which figure represents the result?

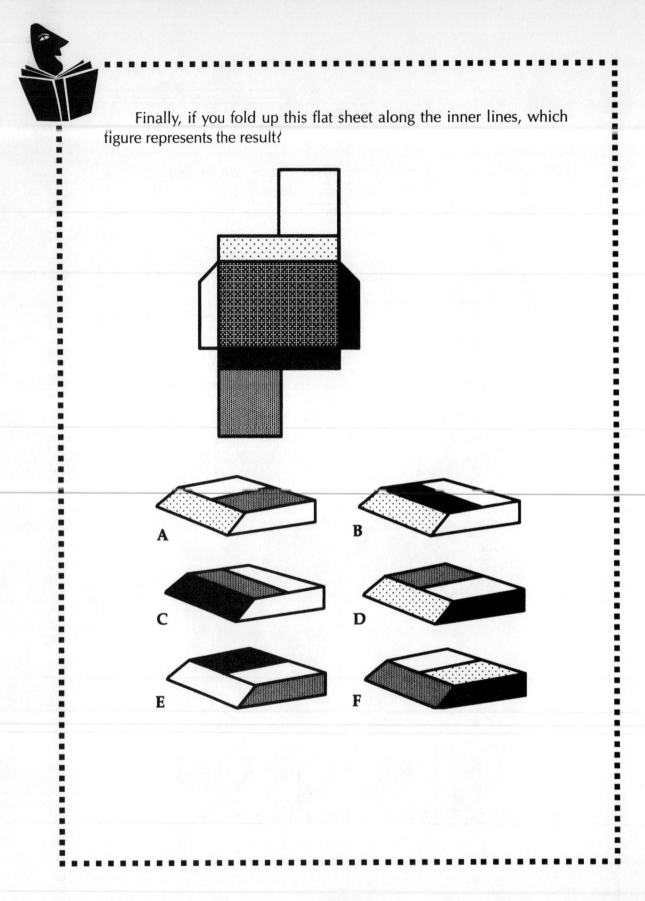

A

B

C

D

E

F

Cut the Cards

Have you ever played cards and wished you had a different hand? Suppose you need a heart instead of a spade. Well, here's your chance to change one suit into another.

Photocopy the spade below. Then use a pair of scissors to cut it into three pieces so that the pieces can be fitted together to form a heart. Can you do it?

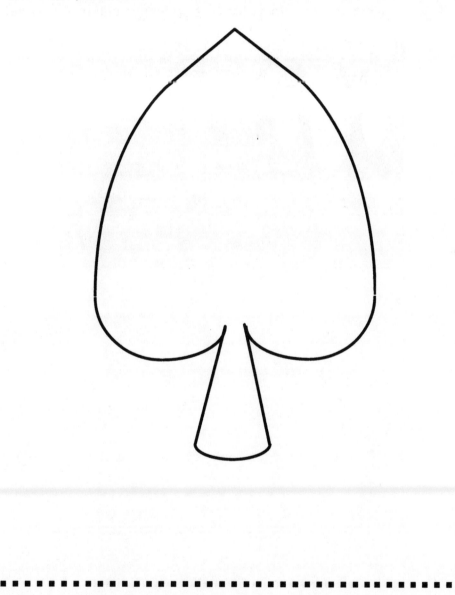

Stripped Stripe

There is a legend about a king who had six brothers and six sisters. His country's flag reflected this family structure with twelve bold stripes. When two of his brothers moved out of the kingdom, the king had two of the stripes removed.

Can you figure out how to cut the flag into as few pieces as possible so that the pieces can be put back together to make the same type of flag, but with two less stripes? No part of the flag can be discarded.

Missing Square

Count the number of blocks that make up this pattern. If you don't want to count each block, you can multiply the number of rows by the number of columns to get a total of sixty-four blocks.

Now photocopy the pattern.

Using a pair of scissors, separate the checkerboard along the inner lines. Reassemble the pieces as shown below.

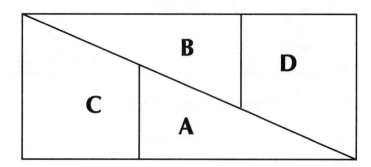

Now count the blocks, or, if you'd rather, just multiply again. The new figure is thirteen blocks long and five blocks high. That gives us sixty-five blocks. Where did the extra block come from?

Tipping the Scales

What whole animal(s) must be added to balance the fourth scale?

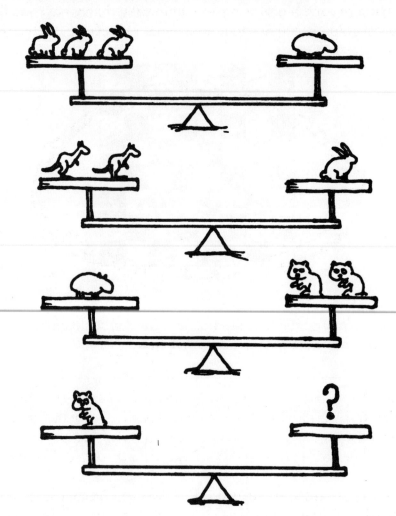

Snake Spread

These hungry snakes are swallowing each other. Since they began this odd dining experience, the circle they formed has gotten smaller. If they continue to swallow each other, what will eventually happen to the circle of snakes?

Falcon Flight

Two bicyclists are situated 60 miles apart. One has a falcon on his shoulder. The bicyclists start riding toward each other at the same time, both maintaining a constant speed of 30 mph. The moment they begin, the falcon flies off the first cyclist's shoulder and toward the other. The falcon flies at a constant ground speed of 45 mph. When the falcon meets the other rider, he reverses direction and flies back to the first cyclist (who is now considerably closer). The falcon continues this back and forth pattern until the riders finally meet. How far did the falcon fly?

A Question of Balance

Place two fingers at the ends of a yardstick. Slowly move the fingers toward each other. As you'll discover, your fingers always meet in the middle of the yardstick.

Now place both fingers in the middle of the stick. Slowly try moving the two of them out to the opposite ends. This time you'll find that one finger remains in the middle while the other moves to the end. Can you explain this behavior?

Well-Balanced Plate

Here's a game that you are guaranteed to win as long as you let your opponent go first. Start with a plate on the exact center of a table. Your opponent must place another plate on the table. Then, it's your turn. During each turn, both of you must continue placing plates until no more plates will fit, but, don't worry, you'll win. Can you figure out the secret?

DOUBLE OR NOTHING ON YOUR ALLOWANCE? OKAY. BUT, YOU GO FIRST.

Robot Walkers

Have you ever seen a robot walker? It is designed to move over various types of terrain so that scientists can use it to explore nearby planets. Our robot walkers are positioned at the corners of a square plot of land. Each robot is programmed to follow the robot directly ahead of it. If all the robots move at the same speed, what will happen to the square pattern? Will the robots ever meet?

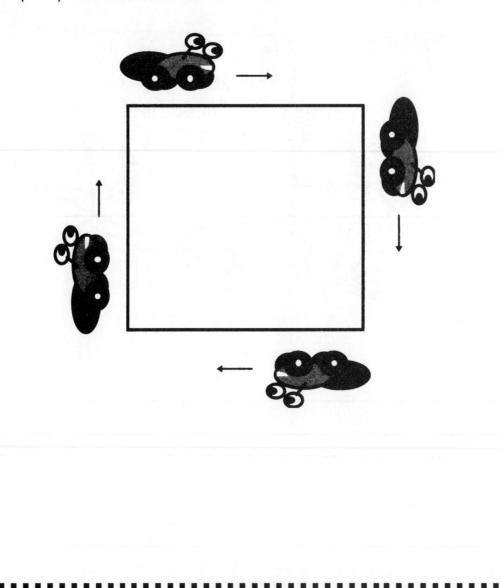

Chain Links

Suppose you own four pieces of chain. One chain has 5 links, two chains have 4 links, and one chain has 3 links.

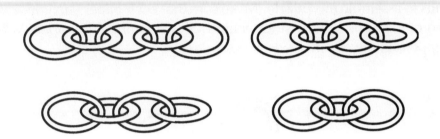

You go to the jeweler and ask her to make a bracelet using all of these chains. She says it would cost $.50 to break a link and $1.00 to weld a link together. You calculate that it would cost $6.00 to build the bracelet. The jeweler, however, says that it would only cost $4.50. Can you figure out how she can assemble your bracelet for less?

Rope Ruse

There is an old legend about an ancient magician who could tie a rope into a knot while holding on to each end of the rope. Can you?

Money Magic

Look at the picture below. Can you guess what will happen when the bill is pulled from both ends?

After you've made your prediction, use a dollar bill and two paper clips to assemble this puzzle. Make sure that each paper clip grips only two of the three side-by-side sections. Slowly pull the bill apart. What happens to the clips? How is it possible?

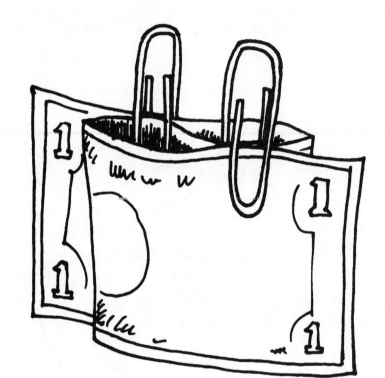

Revolutionary Thoughts

Different things orbit the earth at various speeds and distances. For example, satellites and space instruments released by the space shuttle are only several hundred miles away from the earth, while communications satellites circle at a distance of about 22,300 miles!

In this puzzle, Satellite X-1 orbits our planet once every 9 hours, Satellite Beta once every 4½ hours, and Satellite Parking once every 3 hours.

At time zero, the satellites are positioned in a straight line. How long will it take for all three objects to position themselves again in a straight line?

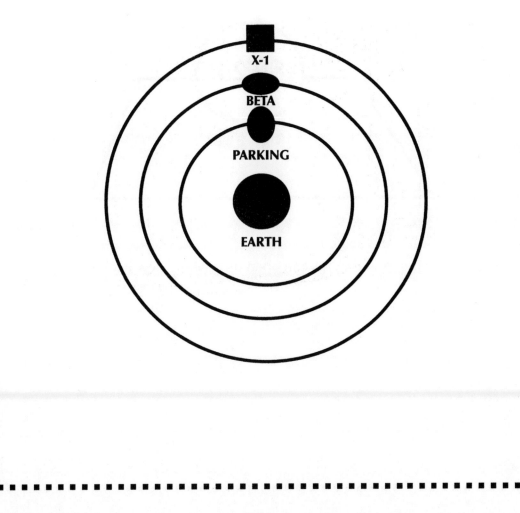

Baffling Holes

Black holes are celestial objects created by collapsed stars. These holes have tremendous concentration of matter and produce such a strong gravitational field that even light can't escape from it. If a black hole was placed on the surface of the earth, our entire planet would be sucked into it!

The hole in this puzzle is not as large as a black hole, but finding its solution can be a big challenge. Do you think a quarter can pass through a hole that is the size of a nickel? You can't tear, cut, or rip the hole. Impossible, you say? Trace the outline of a nickel onto an index card. Carefully cut out this outline.

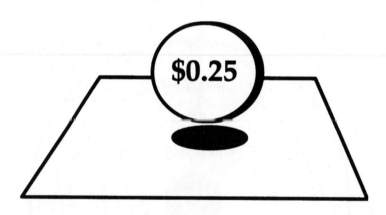

HINT: Bends and twists can open up a whole new geometry.

A Giant Step

Passing a quarter through a nickel-sized hole is nothing when you can step through an index card.

Carefully use a pair of scissors or a modeling knife to cut out the pattern of slots shown here. When you are finished, the hole will open in an accordian-like style and allow you to step through it!

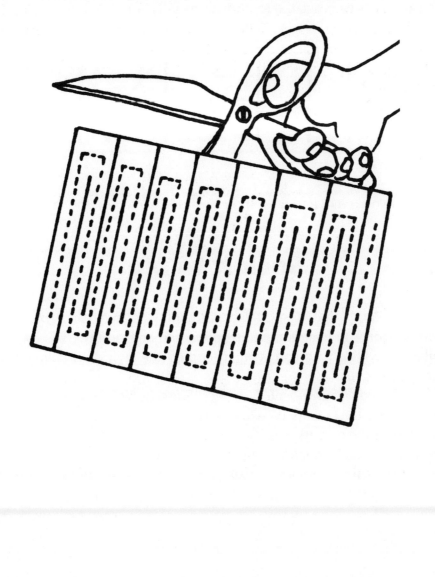

A Fair Solution

Two teenagers are deciding how to share the last piece of pizza. One of them must divide the slice. Both are afraid that the other will cut the slice unfairly and take the larger piece. Can this conflict be resolved by these teenagers so that both will be satisfied by the other one's cut?

After finishing their pizza, the happy teenagers bring out a box of toothpicks and arrange the toothpicks as follows:

Can you remove four toothpicks and leave ten on the table?

Sock It to Me

Did you know that a sock-like garment was first worn by Greek women? This soft leather covering appeared around 600 B.C. and was called a "sykhos." Roman women copied the style and changed the name to "soccus."

Let's open your "soccus" drawer. Suppose you have four pairs of black socks, three pairs of white socks, and a pair of red socks. It is nighttime and you can't see the colors of the socks. You need to select one pair of matching socks. Any color will do.

What is the least number of socks you need to remove from the drawer to ensure that you have at least one matching pair?

Nuts!

When you rotate a bolt clockwise, it travels into the threads of a nut. When that same bolt is rotated counterclockwise, the nut and bolt will separate.

Suppose you have two bolts aligned within each other's threads. If both bolts are rotated clockwise, will they move together, separate, or remain the same distance apart?

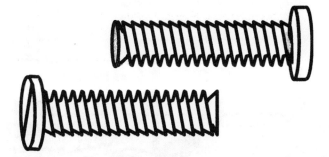

Here's something else to think about. In many large cities, the light bulbs used in places such as subway stations are unique. Instead of screwing into the socket with a clockwise motion, they require counter-clockwise turns. What sense does it make to have these different from most other bulbs?

Doubtful Dimensions

John want to ship a baseball bat to his sister. The bat is 4 feet, 11 inches long. He places it in a rectangular box that is 5 feet long. When he takes it to the shipper, they can't send the package because it is too long. All dimensions of the package must be 4 feet or less in order to be shipped.

When John returns home, he figures out how he can repack the bat. What does he do?

Machine Madness

The identical wheels of this machine are connected by a series of belts. The outer rim of each wheel has a circumference of 8 centimeters. The rim of each wheel's inner shaft has a circumference of 4 centimeters. If the crank is rotated up one-quarter turn, what hour would the clock's hand point to?

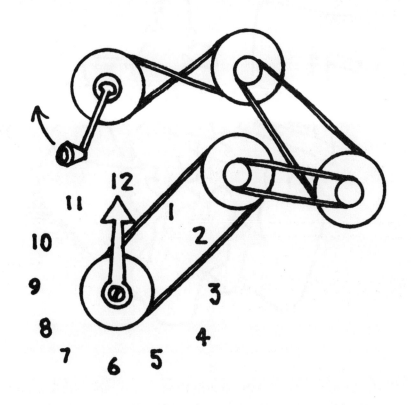

Putting It Together

Suppose you have a list of numbers from one to one hundred. How quickly can you add them all up without using a calculator?

HINT: There is a swift way to add these numbers. Think about how the numbers at the opposite ends of the list relate to each other.

The Heat Is On

The next time you drive under a highway bridge, take a close look at its ends. It is most likely that one end of the bridge will be attached directly to the road. The other end, however, will probably have a small gap. The gap is there on purpose. When the temperature rises, the bridge expands. If the gap wasn't there, the expanding metal bridge might shatter the roadway!

How about holes? Do they also expand when heated? Suppose a metal washer is placed in a flame. What happens to the size of its hole?

City Pipes

Beneath almost every city is an intricate system of large water-carrying pipes. These pipes transport runoff that falls through sewer openings and keep the city streets from flooding when there'a a rainstorm.

The pipes are connected to the surface through manhole openings. Manhole covers fit over the openings. How does their shape prevent them from falling into the hole?

HINT: Think of how the bat from the "Doubtful Dimensions" puzzle on page 48 was packaged!

Magic Square

Take a look a the grid below. Like the "Magic Pyramid" puzzle presented on page 8 of this book, the Magic Square is created when the right numbers are placed in the empty boxes.

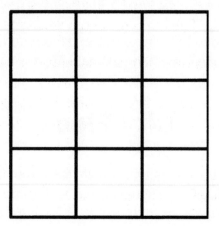

Place a number from 1 to 9 in each of the boxes. Don't repeat any of the numbers. Their arrangement must result in any row of three numbers (vertical, horizontal, or diagonal) adding up to 15.

Anti-Magic Square

Like the Magic Square, the Anti-Magic Square uses the same grid as above, except you have to place the numbers 1 to 9 to create a square where each row's sum is *different*.

Think that's easy? Give it a try. Remember, you can't repeat any of the numbers.

Numbers Game

Here's another game that you're bound to win as long as you let your opponent go first.

The object of the game is simple. The first one to reach 100 wins!

Each round involves adding a number from 1 to 10 to the previous number. Your opponent goes first and identifies a number from 1 to 10. You add to that number and announce the sum. The turns continue until 100 is reached.

The winning strategy is for you to always produce the key numbers, which are 12, 23, 34, 45, 56, 67, 78, 89, and the winning 100.

So if your opponent says 8, you add 4 to get to the first key number 12. You continue adding to the keys, and within nine rounds you'll be a winner.

Now suppose you can only add a number from 1 to 5 to your opponent's number until you reach 50.

What would the key numbers now be?

What's Next?

Take a look at the pattern below. These symbols have a logical order. Can you draw the next symbol in the sequence?

HINT: A little reflection with your thinking skills may help you solve this puzzle.

Connect the Dots

Starting at the top center dot, can you connect all of the other nine dots with only four straight lines? The four lines must all be connected and your pencil can't leave the paper while drawing the answer.

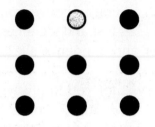

Another Ant Walk

A queen ant finds herself climbing onto the metal framework of a bridge at the spot marked by the arrow.

Can you trace the path she'd need to follow in order to walk across every piece of frame only once and end up at the top of the bridge (marked by an X)?

Her path must be a continuous line.

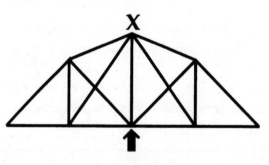

In Order

Examine the set of pictures on the next page. Can you place them in their most logical order?

Tangrams

In Asia, tangrams are known as "the seven plates of wisdom." No wonder, since this Chinese puzzle, probably one of the most famous dissection games, has been around for at least several hundred years.

A tangram consists of five triangles, a square, and a rhomboid.

To get these shapes, copy the lines shown below onto a square sheet of heavy stock paper. Use a pair of scissors to cut out each of the seven sections.

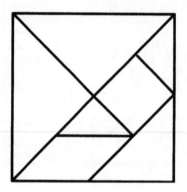

Another way you can make the seven shapes is to start with a square sheet of paper.

1. Cut the square in half to make two large triangles.

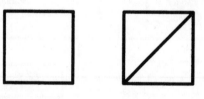

2. Cut one of the triangles in half to make two equal triangles (Sections I and II).

3. Fold back the corner of the other triangle and cut along this fold to get another triangle (Section III).

4. Cut the remaining piece into two equal halves.

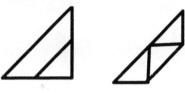

5. Fold and cut one of the pieces to get a square and right triangle (Sections IV and V).

6. Fold and cut the other piece like this (Sections VI and VII).

57

With your seven pieces, try and create these figures.

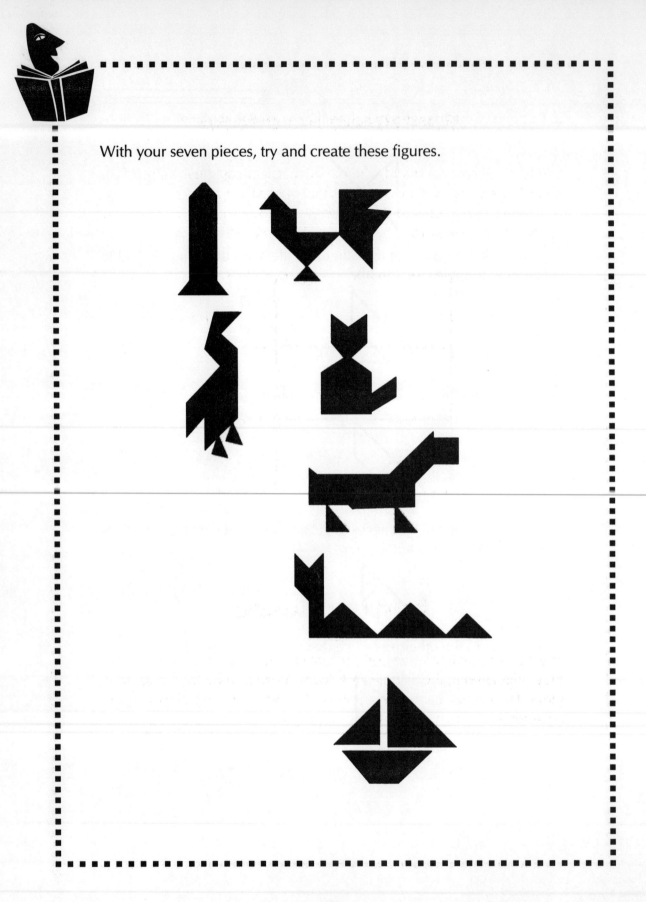

Fractured Farmland

While flying over farmland, a pilot notices the rectangular shape of the fields below. She sketches the lines that divide the fields.

When she returns to the airport, she wonders how many different rectangles can be formed by the lines drawn below?

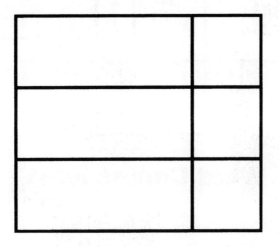

HINT: Don't forget that a square is also a rectangle.

Number Sense

The number symbols we use are called Arabic numerals. Logically, they originated in the Middle East. Right? Wrong. They were created in India. Europeans learned these symbols from Arabic scholars and, inadvertently, the name Arabic numeral stuck.

Now try not to get stuck on this number problem. Can you uncover the logic used to place each of the numbers below? If so, what number should be placed at the question mark?

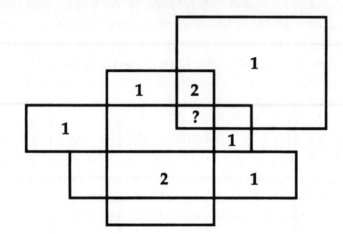

What Comes Next?

Choose the next logical member of the sequence.

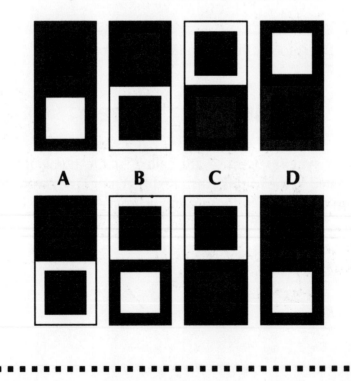

A   B   C   D

The Marked Park

Jethro's custom racer has two different-sized tires. The smaller front tire has a circumference of 7 feet. The larger rear tire has a circumference of 9 feet.

Rita, the meter maid, sees Jethro's racer parked in a 10-minute zone and decides to mark the curbside tires with a spot of paint. She places a mark on the front and rear tires exactly where each tire touches the ground.

Twenty minutes later, Rita returns. She sees both marks still touching the ground. As she begins writing a parking ticket, Jethro returns and explains that he did move his racer. In fact, he moved it the exact distance required to rotate the marks back into their same relative position. Assuming Jethro is telling the truth, what is the shortest distance that the racer was moved?

Pattern Path

All of the numbers below form a sequence. Can you figure out the logic of the sequence? If so, begin at the point marked start and trace a path from box to box. The boxes can be connected horizontally, vertically, or diagonally. Double and triple digit numbers can be made by grouping the numbers this way. You can go through a box only once. Your mission is to finish at the stop sign located in the bottom right corner.

START

2	1	6	4	2	4
8	4	3	2	0	8
6	2	6	1	0	4
1	4	5	5	2	0
2	8	2	1	9	6

Pile Puzzler

Cards can be arranged in many different orders. Don't try all of them unless you have time to count 80,660,000,000,000,000,000,000,000,000, 000,000,000,000,000,000,000,000,000,000,000,000,000.

Here's a card challenge that has fewer solutions. Exchange one card from each of the piles to form three piles with equal sums.

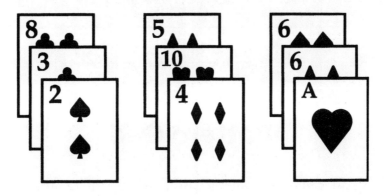

In this puzzle, the Ace only counts as one. Only one card can be exchanged from each pile.

Pattern Puzzler

The five numbers within each circle represent a mathematical relationship. This same relationship is displayed in each of the four circles.

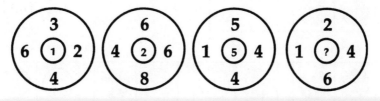

Using this pattern, what is the most likely value for the question mark in the last circle?

Titillating Tiles

There's a tile below that doesn't fit with the other four in the group.
Can you figure out the relationship of the tiles and find the one that is different?

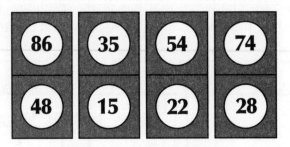

Pattern Grid

A pattern grid is filled with items based on a geometric arrangement to form a visual pattern. Examine the grid below for a pattern and then try to select the section that completes it.

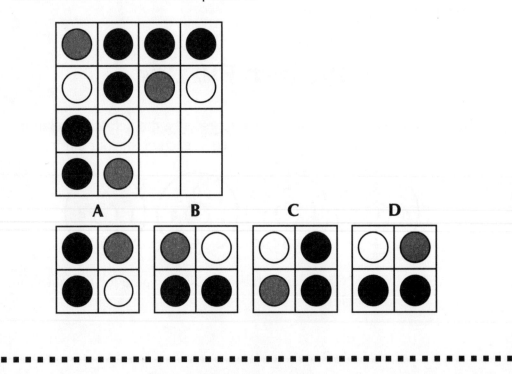

64

ANSWERS

Pyramid Passage

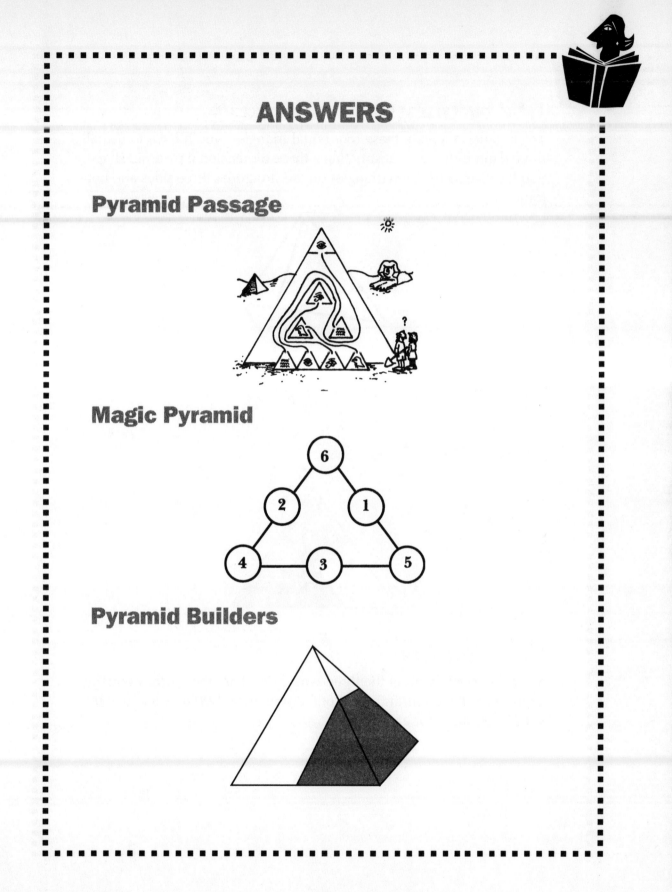

Magic Pyramid

Pyramid Builders

Trial by Triangle

1.   In order to create these four equal triangles, you'll have to use all three dimensions. By constructing a three-dimensional pyramid shape, you'll create same-sized triangles on the structure's three sides and bottom.

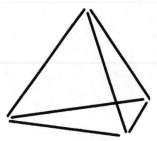

2.   Like the impossible triangle, these two objects are optical illusions and cannot be built.

Trapezoid 2 Triangle

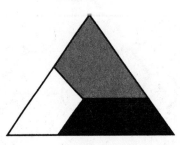

Spare My Brain

Since the four wheels of the three-wheel car share the journey equally, simply take three-fourths of the total distance (50,000 miles) and you'll get 37,500 miles for each tire.

Whirling Paradox

Relative to a stationary observer, the top of the wheel is moving faster than the bottom of the wheel. It all has to do with the forward motion of the car. Since the top half of the wheel is moving in the same direction as the car, their speeds are added together to obtain the relative speed of the moving upper spoke.

However, the lower spokes are moving in the opposite direction as the car. In this case, subtraction of the speeds results in a much slower relative speed—slow enough to count the individual spokes.

Lost?

To find out which way to go, you need to stand the sign back up.

Since you came from Skullara, align the sign so that the Skullara arrow points back to it. All the other arrows will then be pointed to the correct directions.

Sand Traps

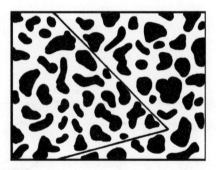

Which Mountain?

It doesn't matter which mountain you climb. All three paths will be the same length. The length of the path is not determined by the shape of the mountain but the slope of the road.

Since all three mountain paths have the same slope, you'd have to walk the same distance in order to climb each 10,000 foot summit.

Compass Caper

White. The bear must be a polar bear. To conform to the given pattern, the hiker must begin the trek at the magnetic North Pole.

A Cut Above

Make two cuts to divide the pizza along its diameter into 4 equal parts. Then stack the quarters on top of each other. Make another cut down the middle of the stack.

Although it might be messy, you'll have eight equal slices.

Kitchen Cups

Fill the three-cup container with water. Pour it into the five-cup container. Fill the three-cup container again, and fill up the five-cup container. This will leave you with exactly one cup of water in the three-cup container.

Moldy Math

This is simpler than it may seem. Since the mold doubles in size every day, it covered half as much area one day before!

And a Cut Below

Eight pieces as shown below:

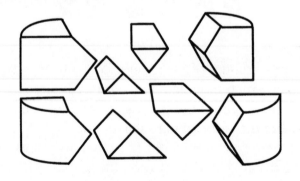

Egg Exactly

Simultaneously turn over the five- and three-minute timers when you begin to boil the water.

When the three-minute timer runs out, put the egg into the boiling water. When the five-minute timer runs out, the egg is done. Two minutes have elapsed.

Losing Marbles?

Start spinning the marble along the bottom of the cup so that it pushes against the inner wall.

When the spin is fast enough, the force overcomes the pull of gravity and the cup can be turned upside down.

A Puzzle of Portions

There are several ways to divide the juice. Here's one of the quickest:

Vessel Size	24	13	11	5
To start	24	0	0	0
First	8	0	11	5
Second	8	13	3	0
Third	8	8	3	5
Fourth	8	8	8	0

Mixed Up?

There is the same amount of root beer in the cola as there is cola in the root beer.

For every drop of root beer that is in the cola cup, a drop of cola has been displaced and is in the root beer cup.

Toothpick Teasers

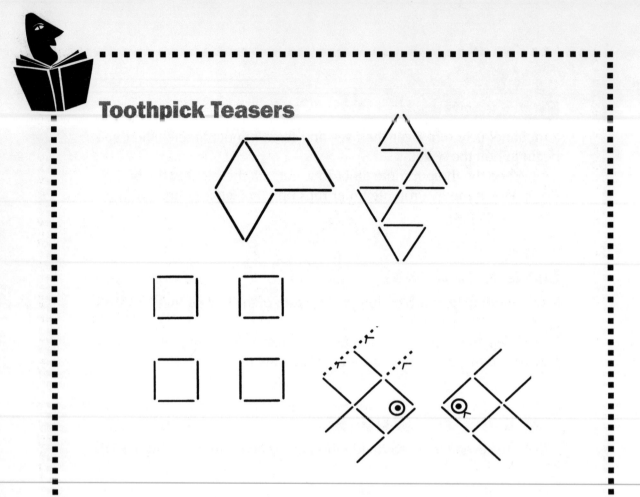

Going to the Movies

Tracing, counting, and remembering each step would drive you crazy. To make things easier, just write down the possible paths to each circle. The number of paths to the next circle is equal to the sum of the paths that connect it.

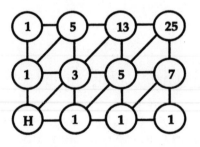

Now Seating?

1. There are ten possible combinations: BBGGG, BGBGG, BGGBG, BGGGB, GBBGG, GBGBG, GBGGB, GGBBG, GGBGB, GGGBB.
2. The chances for two boys being on the ends are 1 in 10.
3. The chances for two girls being on the ends are 3 in 10.

Weighing In...

The weight of the jar doesn't change. In order to fly, the insects must produce downward air currents that are equal in force to their weight. Therefore, whether standing or in flight, the insects push down with the same force.

The Strangest Eyes

Unfortunately, you will need to check this one by tracing over the pattern. As you do, you'll discover a single loop on the left and a double loop on the right.

Monkey Business

Both the crate and the chimp go up.

Head Count

Although this type of problem is perfect for algebra, let's do it visually. If all of the thirty heads belonged to two-legged birds, then there'd be only sixty legs. If one of the animals has four legs, then there'd be sixty-two legs. If two animals are four-legged, there'd be sixty-four legs.

By continuing in this pattern until we reach seventy legs, we will get a combination of twenty-five birds and five lizards.

Möbius Strip

The shape you get from dividing the Möbius strip is one large continuous loop with four twists.

Ant Walk

Nine centimeters. One basic pattern is illustrated below.

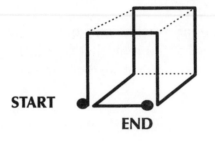

Although there are other turns, they cover the same total length.

Cubic Quandaries

There is a total of 27 cubes. There are six cubes with one red side, twelve cubes with two red sides, eight cubes with three red sides, and one cube with no red sides.

Squaring Off

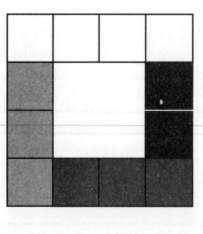

Saving Face

1. The face should have a circle design.

2. The pattern folds into a cube that looks like this:

3. Folding the creases would produce this final version:

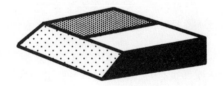

Cut the Cards

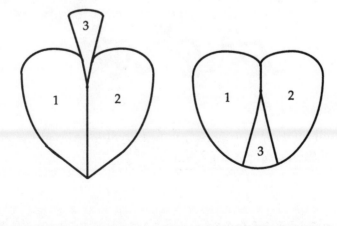

Stripped Stripe

Here is the cut pattern....

and here is the reassembly.

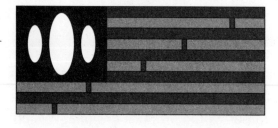

Missing Square

There isn't an extra block. The area making the new block was "shaved off" from some of the other blocks. The loss of each block's area is so small that it's not easy to observe.

Tipping the Scales

Snake Spread

The snakes will fill their stomachs and not be able to swallow anymore. The circle will then stop getting smaller.

Falcon Flight

The falcon's total distance is determined by the amount of time he was aloft and the speed he maintained.

The speed is given. The time is derived from the two cyclists. Since the cyclists are 60 miles apart and drive toward each other at 30 mph, the total time elapsed is 2 hours. The bird flying at 45 miles per hour will cover 90 miles in this 2-hour time period.

A Question of Balance

It has to do with friction, balance, and the weight of the yardstick.

As you move your fingers toward the middle of the yardstick, the balance of the yardstick shifts. The finger that is closer to the middle will support more weight, making it easier for the other, more distant finger to "catch up" and move closer to the middle as well. This "catching up" flip-flops between the two fingers until they both arrive at the middle of the yardstick.

The finger that moves first from the middle immediately bears less of the ruler's weight, which makes it easier for this finger to keep moving. The farther it moves, the easier sliding becomes.

Well-Balanced Plate

You must mirror your opponent's placement of the plate. This way, as long as he has a place for his plate, you have a place for yours.

Robot Walkers

The robots follow a path that forms a continually shrinking and rotating square. Eventually, the robots will meet in the middle of the square.

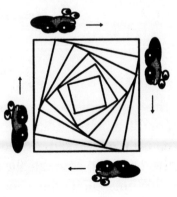

Chain Links

Select the chain with three links. Break open one of the links and use it to connect any two of the other sections. Break another of its links and use it to connect two other sections. Break the third and final link and use it to make a complete loop.

Rope Ruse

Fold your arms as shown below. Then, pick up the free end of the rope while your arms are already crossed. As you uncross your arms, the rope will automatically knot itself.

Money Magic

The clips will lock together and drop off the bill. A paper clip isn't a complete loop. It has two stretched openings through which the clip can slip off the bill. As the two sections of the bill move by each other, the clips slip through their openings and are pushed together to "re-clip" onto each other's loop.

Revolutionary Thoughts

Four and a half hours. In order to be in a straight line the satellites must travel either one full revolution or one-half revolution. In 4½ hours, they'll look like this:

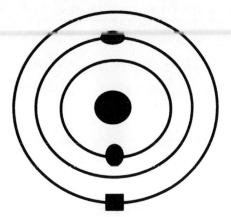

Baffling Holes

Fold the card in half so that the circular hole is also folded in half. Then slightly twist the paper as you pass the quarter snugly through the hole.

A Fair Solution

1. Either teenager can cut the slice, but the other person selects who gets which slice.
2. The four removed toothpicks leave the word "TEN."

Sock It to Me

Four socks. In a worst case scenario, if you draw three socks, each of a different color, the next sock you draw guarantees a matching color.

Nuts!

1. As you rotate each screw in a clockwise direction, they come together.
2. City-owned bulbs have opposite threads so that they won't screw into the standard light sockets that people have in their homes. Therefore, this discourages theft.

Doubtful Dimensions

A box with 3 X 4 dimensions has a diagonal length of 5 feet.

Machine Madness

Midway between 10 and 11 o'clock. The rotation decreases from one-quarter turn to one-eighth turn between the second and third wheel.

As the smaller hub of the second wheel rotates one-quarter turn, it moves the attached belt by only one foot. The 1-foot belt movement spins the larger third wheel only one-eighth of a revolution. This one-eighth turn remains the same for the fourth and fifth wheel. The belt twist between the first and second wheel changes the spin from clockwise to counterclockwise.

Putting It Together

The list contains fifty pairs of numbers that add to 100 (100+0, 99+1, 98+2, 97+3, etc.) with the number 50 as the unpaired leftover. 50 X 100 + 50 = 5,050.

The Heat Is On

As the washer expands, so does the hole it forms. Think of the washer as an image being stretched on a graphics program. Both the washer and its encircled hole will enlarge.

City Pipes

It is impossible for the round sewer cover to fall into the round pipe.

If the cover and tube had rectangular dimensions, the cover would be able to slip into the tube by being tilted in diagonally. But no matter how you tilt the circular cover, it can't fit through a hole of the same dimension.

Magic Square

8	3	4
1	5	9
6	7	2

Anti-Magic Square

5	1	3
4	2	6
8	7	9

Numbers Game

The trick to figuring out the key numbers is to keep subtracting the maximum you can add plus one beginning with the starting number.

For instance, because you can only use the numbers 1-5, if you work in increments 6 down from 50, you will get your key numbers: 8, 14, 20, 26, 32, 38, 44.

What's Next?

The symbols are the mirror images of the numbers 1 to 4 rotated on their sides. The next image is a 5, modified in the same way.

Connect the Dots

The trick to this challenge is that the line can go out of the grid. Otherwise, it is impossible to complete.

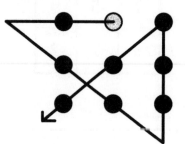

Another Ant Walk

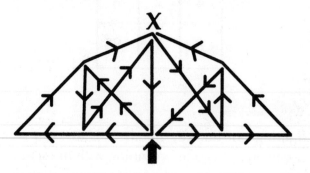

In Order

1. Girl walks to right wearing raingear and umbrella, passes grocery store, in the heavy rain.
2. Girl walks to right, passes record store, wearing raingear and umbrella, in less rain.
3. Girl stops, umbrella up, she holds out hand to feel rain. There is no rain.
4. Girl has stopped, folds up umbrella. There is no rain.
5. Girl walks to left, holds folded umbrella, passes record store. There is no rain.
6. Girl walks to left, holds folded umbrella, passes grocery store. There is no rain.
7. Girl walks to right holding baseball bat, passes grocery store. It is sunny.
8. Girl walks to right, passes record store, holds baseball bat. It is sunny.

Tangrams

81

Fractured Farmland

Eighteen: one whole composite block (1,2,3,4,5,6); six separate blocks (1) (2) (3) (4) (5) (6); three horizontal pairs (1&4) (2&5) (3&6); four vertical pairs (1&2) (2&3) (4&5) (5&6); two vertical triplets (1,2,3) (4,5,6); two large blocks (1,4,2&5) (2,5,3&6)

1	4
2	5
3	6

Number Sense

Three. Each number identifies the numbers of overlapping rectangles that cover that space.

What Comes Next?

D. During each step, the colors advance from outside top to inside top to inside bottom to ouside bottom to outside top.

The Marked Park

Sixty-three feet. The lowest common multiple between the small wheel (7 feet) and large wheel (9 feet) is obtained by multiplying seven and nine.

Pattern Path

The sequence of the path is made by multiplying the digits by two: 2, 4, 8, 16, 32, 64, 128, etc. Here's a small part of that path:

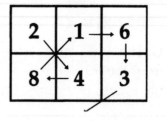

Pile Puzzler

To make things easy, first find the total value for each pile by adding up all the card values. Divide the sum (forty-five) by three to get the value for each pile (fifteen).

10	6	6
2	5	A
3	4	8

Pattern Puzzler

Three. The central number (E) is obtained by dividing the product of the top (A) and bottom (B) numbers by the product of the right (D) and left (C) numbers. A X B/C X D = E.

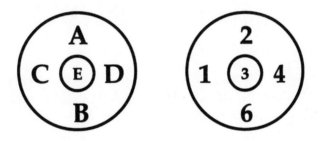

Titillating Tiles

54/22. With the other tiles, when you multiply the individual digits of the top number, you arrive at the bottom number. For example, 4 X 8 = 32.

Pattern Grid

D. The grid is divided into four 4 X 4 tiles. As you go in a "Z" pattern from the top left tile to right to bottom left to right, you'll see that the tile rotates one-quarter turn.

Section 2

GREAT
Critical Thinking
PUZZLES

Introduction

Hang on to your brains because here we go again!

In this section, I present more of the best puzzles for stimulating your critical thinking skills. From mental paths to army ants, you'll encounter an assortment of challenges that are designed to pump up your brain power.

Psychologists and educators refer to critical thinking skills as a variety of higher-level thinking strategies that can be used to analyze, solve, and evaluate all sorts of things, such as facts, theories, statements, and, of course, puzzles. The array of brain-bending puzzles presented in this section should engage many of these skills.

You will have to uncover assumptions, solve by analogy, sequence events, generalize, and discover all sorts of patterns. You will also find yourself digging deeper into your brain to come up with some creative possibilities. Once generated, novel possibilities need to be analyzed in order to determine if they work.

As in section one, there are old-time favorite puzzles with a new twist. For centuries, they have challenged and entertained people. But unbeknownst to the puzzled, these conundrums were also producing new thought channels that had been etched into the cells, chemicals, and electrical patterns of the brain.

Most of the puzzles here can be done with a pencil or pen. Others require simple items, such as loose change or matchsticks, that can be found around the house. But what they all need is for you to be creative and inventive in solving them.

So why wait? Just jump right in and you will be on your way to boosting your critical thinking skills again!

—Michael

Brain Net

Your brain is an incredible piece of machinery. About the size of a squished softball, it contains billions of brain cells. These cells make more connections than all of the phones in the world. It's this huge network that produces your brain power! Want to feel the "brain net" in action?

Take a look at the drawing below. Your job is to figure out how many different paths can get you across from start to finish.

You can only move to the right. You can't go back. When you arrive at a "fork," take either the top or bottom route. Start counting.

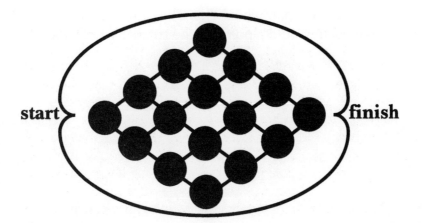

87

Predicting Paths

One of your brain's most powerful capabilities is the ability to think visually. When we think in this way, we construct a mind's eye image of a shape, scene, or concept. This image can be rotated, changed, moved, and analyzed. How good are you at visual thinking? Here's your first chance to find out.

Suppose we roll the wheel along the flat surface. Draw the shape that would be traced by the point within the wheel.

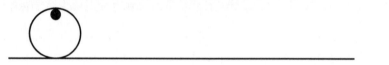

Now let's put the small wheel along the inner rim of a larger circle. What shape path would a point on the smaller wheel trace?

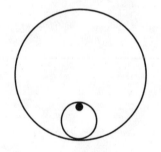

Finally, suppose the inner wheel remains stationary. What pattern would be traced out by a point on the larger rim as it rolls around (and remains in contact with) the inner wheel?

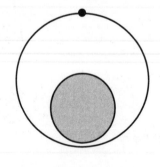

Who's That?

Look into a mirror and who do you see? You? Perhaps, but it's not the same you that everyone else sees. Its a right-left reversed image. The ear that appears on your left side is seen by others on your right side.

Suppose you want to see yourself exactly as others see you. How can you set up two small mirrors so that your reflection isn't reversed?

Leftovers Again?

Your brain is divided into two halves. The left half is more number-oriented, rational, and concrete. Your right half is more creative, play-ful, and artistic. To solve this next puzzle, you'll have to borrow a little from both sides of your brain.

In an art class, students are taught how to shape a 1-ounce bag of clay into a small statue. During this process, some clay remains unused (actually, it falls to the floor). For every five statues that are made, there is enough extra clay to make one more statue. Suppose a student is pre-sented with 25 ounces of clay. What is the maximum number of statues he can sculpt?

Brownie Cut

Now that art class is over, it's time for cooking class.

A chocolate brownie emerges from the oven. Karen cuts the square brownie in half. She then divides one of the halves into two smaller but equal parts.

Before she can eat the larger piece, two of her friends unexpectedly arrive. Karen wants everyone to have the same amount of dessert. In the fewest number of cuts, how can she produce three equal portions?

Balancing Gold

A gold bar balances with nine-tenths of 1 pound and nine-tenths of a similar gold bar. How much does each gold bar weigh?

Thrifty Technique

Don't put that balance away! You'll need it along with a few pounds of brain cells to help solve this next problem.

By the way, did you know that Albert Einstein's brain was "normal" in weight? For the most part, it resembled an ordinary brain. There was, however, a slight difference. He had extra "cleanup" cells (called neuroglial cells). These cells move around the brain to get rid of dead or injured nerve cells. Perhaps his "well-swept" brain supercharged his intelligence?

You have nine gold coins. One of the coins is counterfeit and is filled with a lighter-than-gold substance. Using a balance, what strategy can you use to uncover the counterfeit coin?

To make things a little more difficult, you must identify the fake coin with only two uses of the balance.

Tricky Tide

In the Bay of Fundy, the tides can vary in height by almost 50 feet. The bay in our puzzle has a tidal range of only 6 feet. A boat moors in the middle of this bay. A ladder hangs down from the deck of the boat and touches the flat sea surface. The rungs are 1 foot apart.

At low tide, ten rungs of the ladder are exposed. At high tide, the water level rises 6 feet. How many of the rungs will remain exposed?

Breaking Up Is Hard to Do

How fast can you think? Faster than a speeding bullet? Faster than electricity? For most of us, thoughts race around our brains between 3 to 300 mph. Who knows, this puzzle may break your brain's speed record.

The square encloses a 4 x 4 grid. There are five different ways this grid can be divided into identical quarters. Each way uses a different shape. Can you uncover the layout of all five patterns?

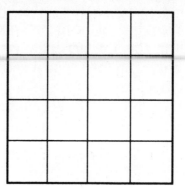

Disorder

Buildings crumble. Living things decompose. It's a scientific principle that things tend to go from order to disorder. The fancy name for this principle is entropy. There are, however, a few things that appear to go against this tendency. Crystals grow and become more complex. Living things take simple chemicals and build complex tissues.

This puzzle, however, uses entropy. Notice how neat and orderly the arrangement of numbers is. Now, let's play the entropy game and rearrange the numbers so that no two consecutive numbers touch each other. They cannot align side by side, up and down, or diagonally.

	1	
2	3	4
5	6	7
	8	

True or False?

Here's a totally different type of problem. This one is based on logic.

Two cultures of aliens live on the planet Trekia, the carpals and the tarsals. The carpals always lie. The tarsals always tell the truth.

A space traveler arrives on Trekia and meets a party of three aliens. She asks the aliens to which culture they belong. The first one murmurs something that is too soft to hear. The second replies, "It said it was a carpal." The third says to the second, "You are a liar!" From this information, figure out what culture the third alien belongs to.

Pack Up Your Troubles

A fragile item is to be shipped in a cardboard box. In order to prevent the item from hitting against the walls of the box, plastic foam cubes are used as "bumpers." There are ten of these cubes. How can you position them along the inner walls of the box so that there is an equal number of cubes along each wall?

Don't Come Back This Way Again!

The pitcher plant is a carnivorous plant that eats insects. An unfortunate insect walks into the pitcher plant's flower. When it tries to reverse direction, it can't. Tiny spines on the petals' surface face downward, which forces the insect to move in one direction—down.

Here's your chance not to go back. The shape below is made with one continuous line. Starting anywhere, can you complete the shape without lifting your pencil from the page? As you probably guessed, your path cannot cross over itself.

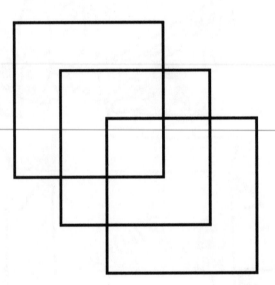

Meet Me on the Edge

Did you know that an ant can lift about fifty times its body weight? If you had that power, you'd be able to lift over 2 tons!

Suppose we position one of those powerful ants on a corner of a sugar cube. On the opposite corner, we position a fly. Suppose the two insects begin walking towards each other. If they can only walk along the edges of the cube (and never go backwards), what is the probability that their paths will cross?

Only the Shadow Knows?

A medium-size jet has a wingspan of 120 feet. An albatross is a bird with a wingspan of about 12 feet. At what altitude would each object have to fly in order to cast shadows of equal size?

More Shadow Stuff

At a certain time of day, a 25-foot telephone pole casts a 10-foot shadow. At that same time, how high would a tree have to be in order to cast a 25-foot shadow?

Trip Times

Did you know that the speed record for cars is over 700 miles per hour? To attain this supersonic speed, the cars use rocket engines. They move so quickly that if the car body had wings, the vehicle would fly!

The car in our problem is much slower. In 1 hour, traveling at 30 mph, it climbs to the top of the hill. When the car reaches the top, the driver remembers that she left her field guide to mountain life back home. She immediately turns around and drives downhill at 60 mph. Assuming that she spent no time at the top, what was her average speed?

HINT: It is not 45 mph.

Average Puzzle

How fast can you ride a bicycle? To get into the *Guinness Book of Records* for human-powered cycling, you'd need to ride faster than 60 mph.

An ordinary cyclist travels up and down a hill. Going up, she maintains a constant speed of 10 mph. It takes her 1 hour to get to the top. Assuming that the hill is symmetric, what speed must she maintain on the way going down if she wishes to average 20 mph? Before you bask in victory, the answer is not 30 mph.

Palindrome

A palindrome is a word or number that reads the same backwards as it does forward. Numbers such as 606 and 4334 are palindromes.

While driving his car, Bob (so much of a palindrome lover that he changed his name from John to Bob) observes that the odometer reading forms a palindrome. It displays the mileage 13,931.

Bob keeps driving. Two hours later, he looks at the odometer again and, to his surprise, it displays a different palindrome!

What is the most likely speed that Bob is traveling?

Stacking Up

Can you arrange these numbered blocks into three equal stacks so that the sum of the numbers displayed in each stack must be equal to any other stack.

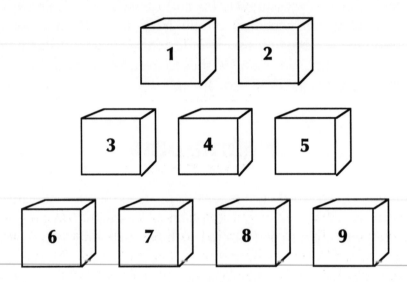

Star Birth

Trace this octagon pattern onto a separate sheet of paper. Then decide how to divide this shape into eight identical triangles that can be arranged into a star. The star will have eight points and an octagon-shaped hole in its center. When you think you've come up with an answer, trace the pattern onto the octagon. Cut out the separate parts and reassemble them into a star.

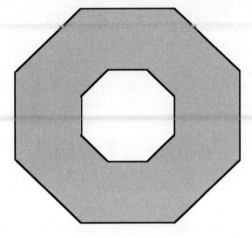

Flip Flop

Did you know that the ancient Egyptians believed that triangles had sacred qualities? This may have led to the superstition about walking under a ladder. When a ladder is placed against a wall, it forms a triangle. To walk through the triangle might provoke the wrath of the gods.

   The triangle below is made up of ten disks. Can you move three of the disks to make the triangle point in the opposite direction?

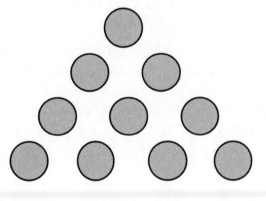

Crossing Hands

Picture in your mind a clock with a face and hands. Between the hours of 5 AM and 5 PM, how many times will the hour and minute hands cross each other?

What's Next?

Examine the figures below. Can you see what the pattern is and find out what the fourth figure in this series should look like?

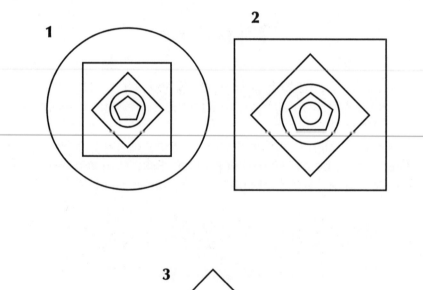

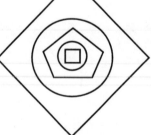

Trying Triangles

How many triangles can be found in this figure?

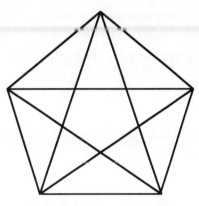

Flipping Pairs

Place three coins with their indicated side facing up as shown. In three moves, arrange the coins so that all three have the same side facing up. A move consists of flipping *two* coins over to their opposite side.

NOTE: Flipping the pair of outer coins three times doesn't count!

Missing Blocks

Examine the figure of blocks below. Let's assume that the hidden blocks are all in place. How many additional blocks are needed to fill in the empty region to complete this cube?

Once you've made your guess, look at the pattern again. Assume that the hidden blocks are all in place. Now let's suppose that all of the blocks you can see are vaporized. How many blocks would be left behind?

Matchstick Memories

Years ago, matchsticks were made from small sections of wood. These common and inexpensive objects were perfect props for after-dinner or parlor room activities. Nowadays, toothpicks offer the same advantages. So get your picks together and arrange them in the three patterns shown below.

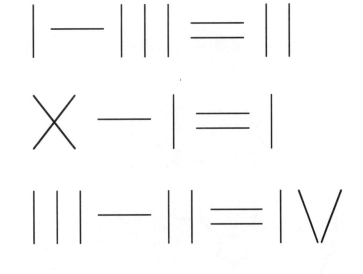

As you can see, each line of matchsticks forms an incorrect equation. The challenge is to make each one correct by changing the position of only one of the matchsticks in each row.

Sum Circle

Place the numbers one through six within the six smaller circles shown below. Each number must be used only once. The numbers must be placed so that the sum of the four numbers that fall on a circle's circumference is equal to the sum of the numbers on any other circle's circumference.

Think it's easy? Give it a try.

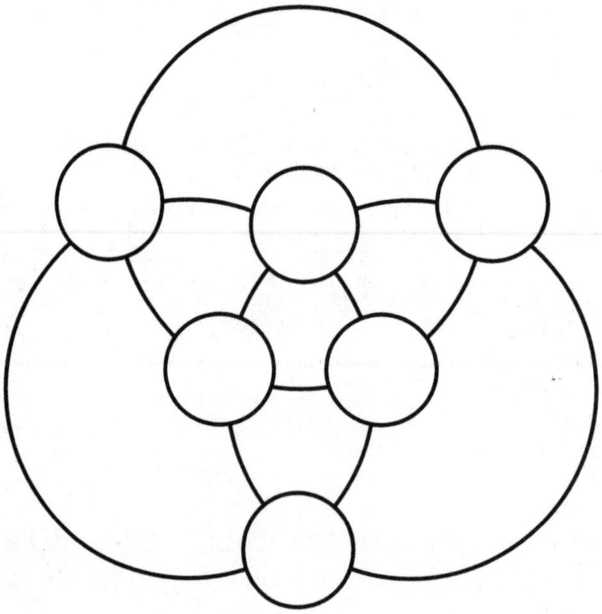

Many Rivers to Cross

Let's take a break from puzzles and go on a rowboat ride across the river. There are four adults who want to cross it. They come upon a boy and a girl playing in a rowboat. The boat can hold either two children or one adult. Can the adults succeed in crossing the river? If so, how?

Train Travel

A train travels at a constant rate of speed. It reaches a stretch of track that has fifteen poles. The poles are placed at an equal distance to each other. It takes the train 10 minutes to travel from the first pole to the tenth pole. How long will it take the train to reach the fifteenth pole?

Miles Apart

The distance from New York to Boston is 220 miles. Suppose a train leaves Boston for New York and travels at 65 mph. One hour later, a train leaves New York for Boston and travels at 55 mph. If we assume the tracks are straight paths and the trains maintain a constant speed, how far apart are the trains 1 hour before they meet?

Passing Trains

Coming from opposite directions, a freight train and a passenger train pass each other on parallel tracks. The passenger train travels at 60 mph. The freight train travels at 30 mph. A passenger observes that it takes 6 seconds to pass the freight train. How many feet long is the freight train?

HINT: There are 5,280 feet in a mile.

Souped-Up Survey

A survey agency reported their results in the local newspaper. The report states that exactly one hundred local lawyers were interviewed. Of the one hundred, seventy-five lawyers own BMWs, ninety-five lawyers own Volvos, and fifty lawyers own both a BMW and a Volvo.

Within a short time after the report, several lawyers argue that the survey results are incorrect. How can they tell?

Toasty

In order to make French toast, Ricardo must fry both sides of a bread slice for 30 seconds. His frying pan can only hold two slices of bread at once. How can he make three slices of French toast in only 1½ minutes instead of 2 minutes?

Circle Game

Examine the pattern of circles below. Can you place the numbers one through nine in these circles so that the sum of the three circles connected vertically, horizontally, or diagonally is equal to fifteen?

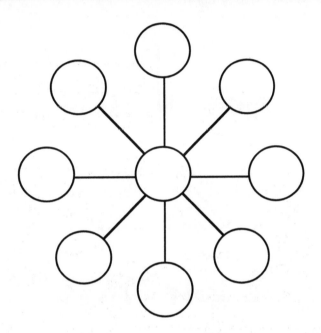

A Fare Split

Michelle rents a car to take her to the airport in the morning and return her home that evening. Halfway to the airport, she picks up a friend who accompanies her to the airport. That night, she and her friend return back to Michelle's home. The total cost is $20.00. If the amount to be paid is to be split fairly, how much money should Michelle pay?

Pentagon Parts

The pentagon below is divided into five equal parts. Suppose you color one or more parts gray. How many different and distinguishable patterns can you form? Each pattern must be unique and not be duplicated by simply rotating the pentagon.

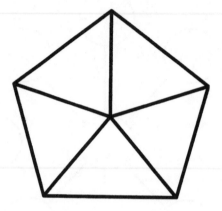

Bagel for Five?

You and four friends have decided to split a bagel for breakfast. The five of you are not fussy about the size of the piece each will receive. In other words, all the pieces don't have to be the same size.

Using two perfectly straight cuts, is it possible to divide this bagel into five pieces?

Coin Moves

Place twelve coins in the pattern shown below. Notice how they form the corners of six equal-sized squares. Can you remove three of the coins to have only three equal-sized squares remaining?

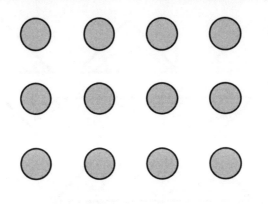

Trapezoid Trap

Divide the trapezoid below into four identical parts.

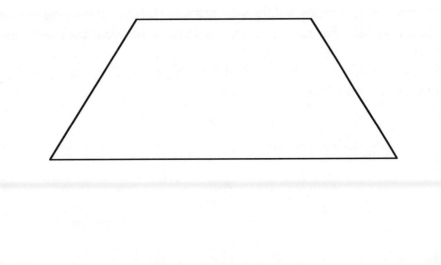

A+ Test

Here's a math challenge of a different sort. Trace these five shapes onto a sheet of stiff paper. Use a pair of scissors to carefully cut them out. Then assemble the shapes into a "plus" sign.

Mis-Marked Music

There are three boxes filled with audiocassette tapes. One box contains rap tapes, another contains jazz tapes, while the third contains both rap and jazz tapes. All three boxes have labels identifying the type of tapes within. The only problem is that all of the boxes are mislabeled.

By selecting only one box and listening to only one tape, how can you label all three boxes correctly?

Measuring Mug

Without the aid of any measuring device, how can you use a transparent 16-ounce mug to measure a volume of water that is exactly 8 ounces?

Coin Roll

Two identical coins are positioned side by side. In your mind's eye, roll the coin on the left (Coin A) over the other coin (Coin B). When Coin A reaches the opposite side of Coin B, stop. In which direction will Coin A's head be facing?

Now, let's suppose that Coin A rolls completely around Coin B. If so, how many rotations does Coin A make around its own center?

Painting on the Side

You are presented with several white cubes and a bucket of red paint. To make each of them different, you decide to paint one or more sides of each cube red. How many distinguishable cubes can you make with this painting method? Remember that any painted side must be painted completely to make it indistinguishable from any other painted side.

Magic Triangle

Here's a magic triangle whose sides are formed by sets of four numbers. To solve the puzzle, place the numbers one through nine each in one of the circles. When you are finished, the sums of all three sides must be equal.

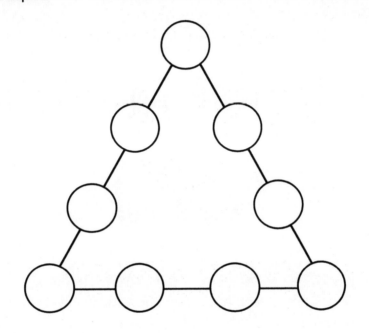

There are three different sums that can be used to reach the solution. Can you find all three?

Patterns

The arrangement of numbers below represents a pattern. This pattern is a mathematical relationship between the numbers in each square, so don't look for things like spelling, days of the week, cryptograms, or codes. Can you uncover the pattern and fill in the question mark in the last square?

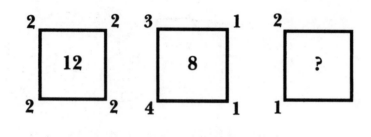

Frog Jump

A frog falls into a well that is 18 feet deep. Every day the frog jumps up a total distance of 6 feet. At night, as the frog grips the slimy well walls, it slips back down by 2 feet. At this rate, how many days will it take the frog to jump to the rim of the well?

Army Ants

Two small armies of ants meet head-on along a jungle path. Both armies would prefer to pass each other rather than fight. There is a small space along the side of the path. It is only large enough to hold one ant at a time. Is it possible for the armies to pass each other? If so, how?

No Sweat

There are six players on a coed volleyball team. After an exhausting game, each girl drinks 4 cups of water. Each boy drinks 7 cups of water. The coach drinks 9 cups.

A total of 43 cups of water is consumed by everyone. How many boys and how many girls are on the team?

Go Figure!

In a distant planet, there are four forms of life beings: zadohs, pugwigs, kahoots, and zingzags. All zadohs are pugwigs. Some pugwigs are kahoots. All kahoots are zingzags.

Which of the following statement(s) must then be true?

1. Some zadohs are zingzags.
2. Some kahoots are zadohs.
3. All kahoots are pugwigs.
4. Some zingzags are pugwigs.
5. All zingzags are zadohs.
6. Some zadohs are kahoots.

Square Pattern

Suppose you have to paint all nine squares in the grid below using one of three colors: red, blue, or green. How many different patterns can you paint if each color must be represented in every row and every column? Each pattern must be unique. In other words, a new pattern can't be made by simply rotating the grid.

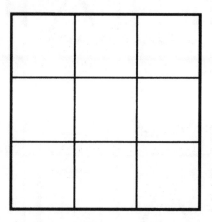

Bouncing Ball

Did you know that when a ball strikes the ground, its shape distorts? This distortion stores the energy that powers its rebound. The more its shape changes, the higher the ball will bounce.

The ball in this puzzle rebounds to half the height from which it is dropped. Suppose it is dropped from a 1-meter height. What distance would the ball travel before it comes to rest?

Complete the Pattern

Use the pattern below to determine the value for X and Y.

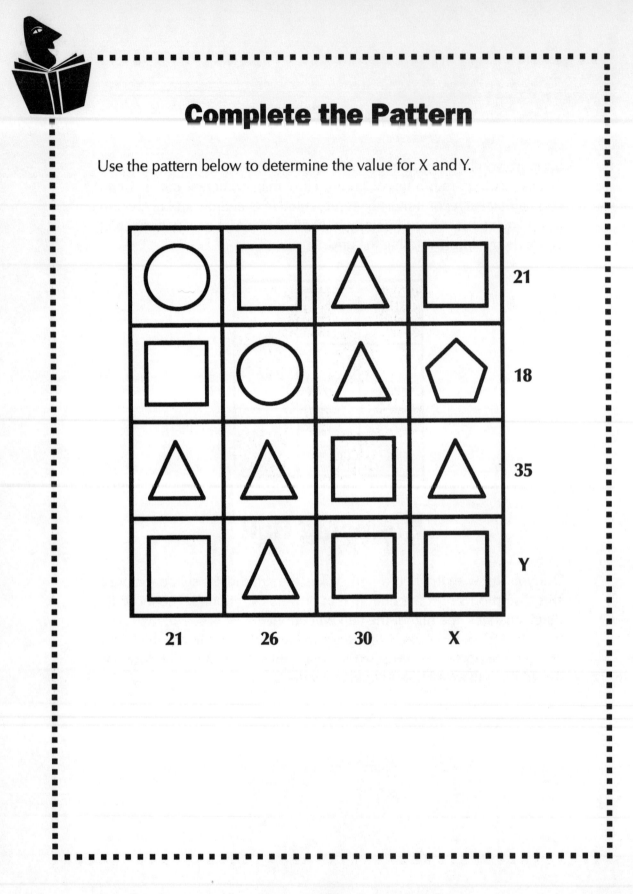

Checkerboard

A full-size checkerboard has eight rows and eight columns that make up its sixty-four squares. By combining the patterns of these squares, you can put together another 140 squares. The pattern below is one-fourth the area of a full size checkerboard. What is the total number of squares that are found in this smaller pattern?

Cutting Edge

Kristin wants to remodel her home. To save money, she decides to move a carpet from one hallway to another. The carpet currently fills a passage that is 3 x 12 feet. She wishes to cut the carpet into two sections that can be joined together to fit a long and narrow hallway that is 2 x 18 feet. What does her cut look like?

The Die Is Cast

Which die is unlike the other three?

Playing with Matches?

Thirty-two soccer teams enter a statewide competition. The teams are paired randomly in each round. The winning team advances to the next round. Losers are eliminated. How many matches must be played in order to crown one winner?

Competing Clicks

Let the Mouse Click Competition Begin!

Emily can click a mouse ten times in 10 seconds. Buzzy can click a mouse twenty times in 20 seconds. Anthony can click a mouse five times in 5 seconds. Assume that the timing period begins with the first mouse click and ends with the final click. Which one of these computer users would be the first to complete forty clicks?

Another Pattern

Here is another mathematical pattern that relates the four numbers of each triangle. Can you uncover the pattern and use it to complete the third triangle?

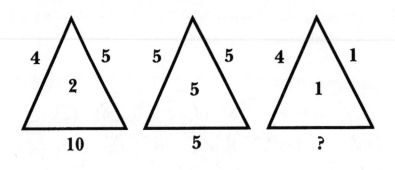

Vive le Flag

The French tricolor flag is made up of three vertical stripes: red, white, and blue. Suppose you are given four different colors of fabric and asked to create a different flag using the same tricolor design. If no two adjacent stripes can be the same color, how many different combinations of color patterns are there?

HINT: Don't forget that the flag pattern can be flipped over!

Pizza Cut

Five people want to share a square pizza. The first person (who is really hungry) removes a quarter of the pie. When the others find out, they are annoyed and try to divide the remaining three-fourths into four equal and identically shaped slices. The cuts must be straight. How must they cut the remaining pizza in order to produce four identical slices?

Slip Sliding

For this challenge, you'll need to get seven coins. Place a coin on any of the star's eight points. Then slide the coin along one of the straight lines to its endpoint. Place a second coin on another point. Slide this one down to its endpoint. Continue in this manner until all seven coins have been placed.

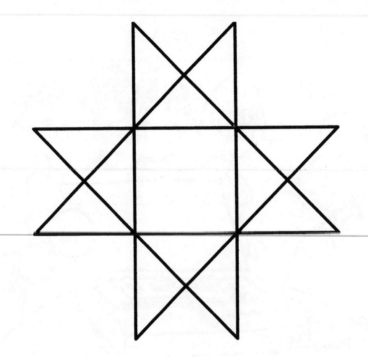

NOTE: It can be done—but you'll need to develop a strategy.

A, B, See?

Each letter stands for a different digit in each equation. Can you decode each one?

AB	AA	ABA	ABA
xAB	+AA	+BAB	+BAA
ABB	BBC	BBBC	CDDD

Spare Change

Jonathan has a pocket full of coins. Yet he doesn't have the right combination of coins to make change for a nickel, dime, quarter, half dollar, or dollar.

What is the largest value of coins Jonathan can have in his pocket?

Puzzling Prices

A puzzle book costs $5.00 plus one-half of its price. How much does the puzzle book cost?

HINT: It's more expensive than this book.

Gum Drop

In preparation for a party, Heather fills a large jar with gum drops. Before the party begins, Michael sees the gum drop jar. He (hoping that no one will realize) takes one-third of the drops. Soon after, Tanya takes one-third of the gum drops (she, too, hopes that no one will notice). Finally, Britt appears and, like the others, she takes one-third of the gum drops. If forty gum drops are left in the jar, how many did it originally contain?

Go-Cart Crossing

Three go-cart tracks are built as shown. Each track forms a separate one-third of a mile loop. Three go-carts begin riding at the same time from the central point where all three tracks cross. One go-cart travels at 6 mph, another at 12 mph, and the third at 15 mph. How long will it take for all three go-carts to cross paths for the fifth time?

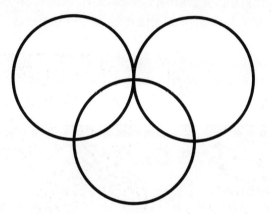

Table Manners

Four couples enter a restaurant. How many ways can they be seated at a round table so that the men and women alternate and no husband and wife sit next to each other?

Winning Slip

A contest is fixed. Everyone knows it, including the contestants. One of the contestants, however, makes it to the final playoff level.

The master of ceremonies presents the following challenge: "This box contains two slips of paper. One slip has the word 'winner' printed on it, the other has the word 'loser.' Your task is to select the winning slip—without looking, of course."

The contestant knows that this challenge is fixed. He realizes that both slips have the word "loser." How can he select one slip and win the challenge? By the way, the contestant can't declare this contest is a fraud or he'd lose his current winnings.

Ancient Man

An ancient Greek was said to have lived one-fourth of his life as a boy, one-fifth as a youth, one-third as a man, and spent the last 13 years as an elderly gent. How old was he when he died?

Lights Out!

The total output of electrical energy from your brain is only about 20 watts. That's not an avalanche of power (especially when you consider that most household light bulbs use five times that amount). Now try powering up with this problem.

Imagine that you can't sleep because you are kept awake by the flashing neon lights that shine through a square store window. The window measures 10 x 10 feet.

A friend assures you that he can cover up half the area of the window but still leave a square section that is 10 x 10 feet. This will then satisfy both you and the storekeeper. You think your friend has lost it. Has he?

Pencil Puzzle

Can you uncover the logic used to create this layout? If so, use that same logic to determine the letter for the question mark.

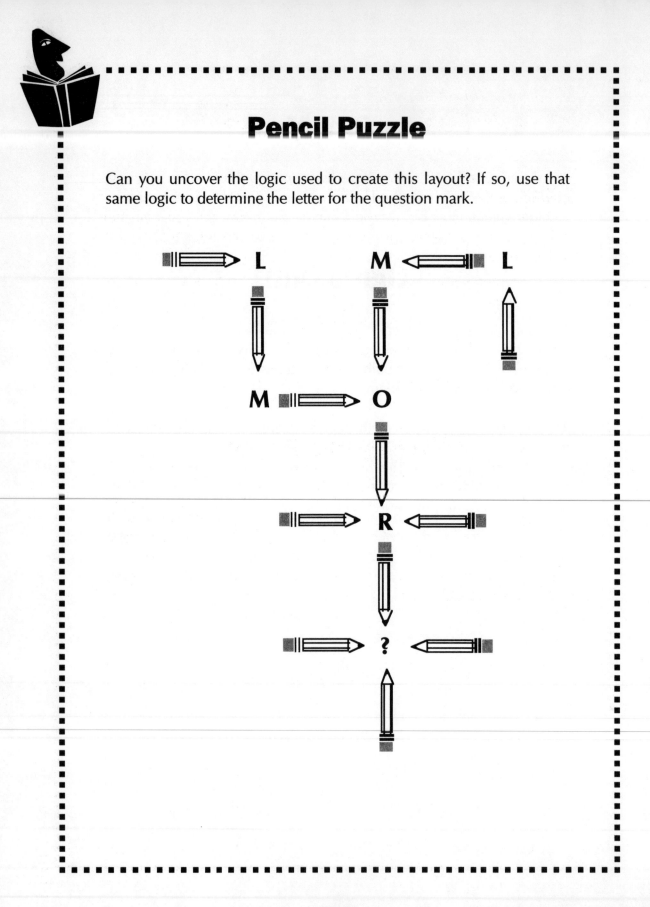

Sounds Logical?

It's the weekend! Saturdays and Sundays are the days that Sheila, Ramon, and Niko shop together for music. The CDs they purchase are either rock 'n' roll or jazz. When they visit the music store, each person will purchase one and only one CD. Here are the rules that govern their selections.

1. Either Sheila or Ramon will pick rock 'n' roll, but not both of them.
2. If Sheila picks rock 'n' roll, Niko picks jazz.
3. Niko and Ramon do not both pick jazz.

Which one of the three purchased a jazz CD on Saturday and a rock 'n' roll CD on Sunday?

Triangular Tower

Suppose ten billiard balls are placed in the standard triangular rack. If additional billiard balls are placed on top of this pattern, some balls will roll into the gullies to form a smaller, stable triangle (forget about the balls which roll off the stack). If you add more layers, you'll eventually build a billiard ball pyramid. How many billiard balls and levels would the pyramid contain?

Criss-Crossed

Place six coins in the layout as shown below. Notice that this arrangement forms two columns. The horizontal column has four coins. The vertical column has three coins. Can you move only one coin to form two columns with each containing four coins?

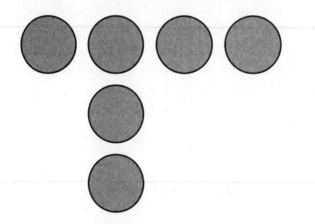

Crystal Building

Have you ever looked closely at a crystal? If so, you may have noticed that the crystal has flat sides and uniform angles. That's because a crystal is a repeating arrangement of tiny particles of matter. Often, a central particle is surrounded on all sides by other particles. Here's a puzzle that will help you visualize a crystal pattern.

Suppose you coat a tennis ball with glue. What is the maximum number of tennis balls that can attach directly to this sticky surface?

Testy Target

Ten arrows are shot at the target below. One of them misses the target completely. The others all strike it. If the total sum of points is one hundred, in which part of the target did each arrow strike?

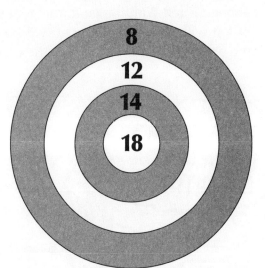

Eighth-Century Enigma

Here's a puzzle that can be traced back to the eighth century. A man has a goat, a wolf, and a head of cabbage. He comes to a river and must bring these three things across to the other side. The boat can only take the man plus either the goat, wolf, or cabbage. There is another problem. If the cabbage is left with the goat, the goat will eat the cabbage. If the wolf is left with the goat, the goat will be devoured. How can he transport the wolf, goat, and cabbage to the other side?

Planet Rotation

Our planet spins counterclockwise on its axis. It also has a counter-clockwise revolution around the sun. Suppose both motions now go clockwise. How would this affect the apparent direction of sunrise and sunset?

Shuffle

Pretend you have five cards: a ten, a jack, a queen, a king, and an ace. In your mind's eye, shuffle these five cards together and put the pile face down. If you were to select four cards, returning each card and reshuffling the deck after each pick, what kind of hand would you more likely draw: four Aces or a straight picked in sequence? Can you explain why?

Some Exchange

The first written puzzles appeared in ancient Egypt at about 1650 B.C. These puzzles were part of an 18½-foot scroll called the Rhind Papyrus. Times have changed since then, but many puzzles haven't. Just try these next ones.

Examine the two stacks of number blocks. If you exchange one block from one column with one block from the other, the number of their sums will be equal. Which blocks need to be exchanged?

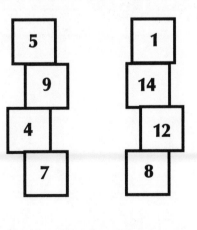

Now that you know how to balance two columns, you're ready to move up to three columns! By exchanging one block from each column, each of the three blocks' sums will be equal. Remember that all three columns must undergo only one exchange.

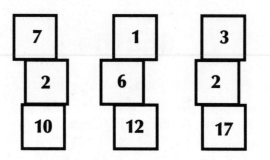

ANSWERS

Brain Net

Twenty routes. Although you can chart them all out, there is a less confusing way. Starting at the left, identify the number of routes that can get you to a circle. You can arrive at this number by adding the numbers found in the connecting circles to the left. Keep going until you get to the finish.

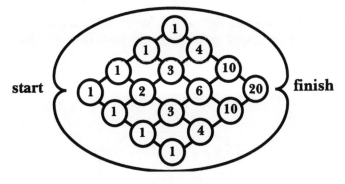

Predicting Paths

a.

b.

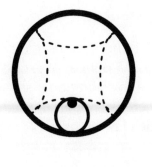

c.

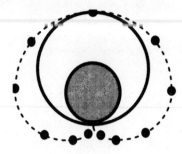

Who's That?

Position the mirrors so that they are arranged like an opened book. The right side of your face will reflect on the right side of the mirror. This image does not reflect back to that eye. Instead, it bounces to the other mirror. From there, the image is reflected back to the other eye.

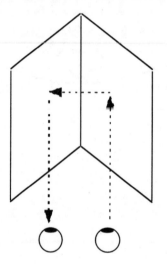

Leftovers Again?

Thirty-one statues. The 25 ounces are used directly to make twenty-five statues. During this process, 5 ounces of excess clay are produced. This extra clay is used to make five additional statues. While making these five additional statues, there is enough unused clay to make one more statue with one-fifth of the clay left over.

Brownie Cut

One cut

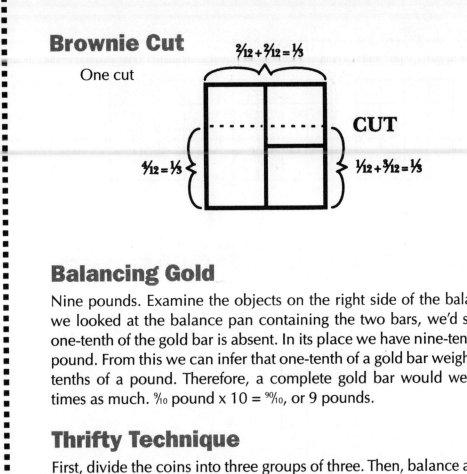

$2/12 + 2/12 = 1/3$

CUT

$4/12 = 1/3$

$1/12 + 3/12 = 1/3$

Balancing Gold

Nine pounds. Examine the objects on the right side of the balance. If we looked at the balance pan containing the two bars, we'd see that one-tenth of the gold bar is absent. In its place we have nine-tenths of a pound. From this we can infer that one-tenth of a gold bar weighs nine-tenths of a pound. Therefore, a complete gold bar would weigh ten times as much. $9/10$ pound x 10 = $90/10$, or 9 pounds.

Thrifty Technique

First, divide the coins into three groups of three. Then, balance any one group against another group. If the counterfeit is contained in either of the groups, the coins will not balance. If, however, they balance, the counterfeit coin must be in the third pile. Now that we have identified the pile with the counterfeit coin, remove one coin from the pile and balance the other two. The lighter coin will not balance. If the two coins do balance, the counterfeit coin is the one not selected.

Tricky Tide

Five rungs will still remain exposed. As the tide comes in, the boat will rise up.

Breaking Up Is Hard to Do

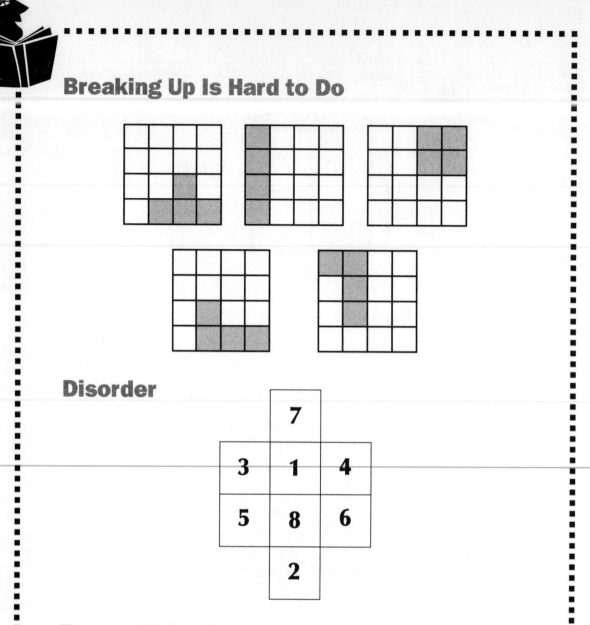

Disorder

	7	
3	1	4
5	8	6
	2	

True or False?

Tarsal. To figure this one out, we need to look at each alien's response. If the first alien was a tarsal, it would identify itself as a tarsal. If it was a carpal, it would still identify itself as a tarsal. Either way, the mumbling alien would identify itself as a "tarsal." Therefore, the second alien had to be lying. The third alien truthfully identified the carpal, making him a truth-telling tarsal.

Pack Up Your Troubles

The "trick" is using the same block in the rows of two adjacent sides.

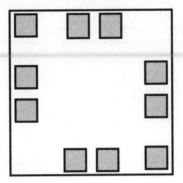

Don't Come Back This Way Again!

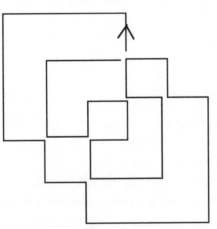

Meet Me on the Edge

One in six. The ant (or fly) can take any one of the six available routes. It doesn't matter.

Now, the other insect must select the "collision route" from its own six possible choices. Therefore, the odds are one in six.

Only the Shadow Knows?

They can never cast shadows of equal size.

Any difference in their altitude would be negligible compared to their distance from the sun. It's those 93,000,000 miles from our planet to the sun that affect the shadows' size much more than their puny distances apart.

More Shadow Stuff

At that time of day, the shadow is two-fifths of the object's height. If the tree's shadow (two-fifths of the unknown height) is 25 feet, then the height of the tree is 62½ feet.

Trip Times

Since it takes her 1 hour to reach the top (while traveling at 30 mph), the hill is a 30-mile route. Traveling at 60 mph, she'll cover that distance in only 30 minutes.

The average speed is the total distance/total time = 60 miles/1.5 hours or 40 mph.

Average Puzzle

There is no way that she can average 20 mph for the whole trip. Like the uphill path, the downhill path is only 10 miles. This distance is too short to achieve an average speed (for the whole trip) of 20 mph.

Consider this: If she completed her trip by traveling the downhill path at 600 mph, then her average speed would be the total distance divided by the total time, or 20 miles/61 minutes, or an average of about 19.6 mph.

By examining this equation, you'll see that there will be no way for her to decrease the denominator (time) below the 60 minutes she has already spent cycling up the hill.

Palindrome

55 mph. The next palindrome that the odometer can display is 14,041. To reach this value, Bob will have had to travel 110 miles. If it took him 2 hours to reach this point, his average speed will be 55 mph.

All other palindromes would have required too many miles to produce a logical speed. For example, the odometer's next palindrome is 14,141. From this, you can calculate an average speed of 105 mph—highly unlikely.

Stacking Up

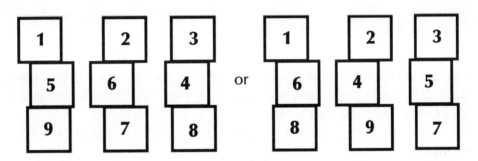

Star Birth

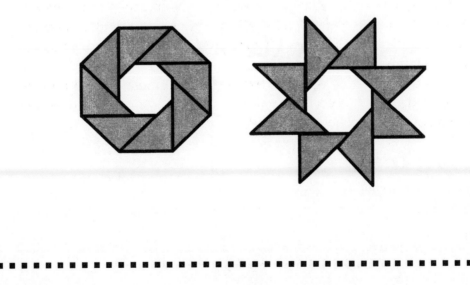

Flip Flop

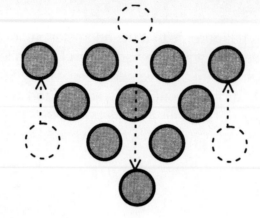

Crossing Hands

Eleven times. For each hour up until 11:00, the clock's hands will cross once. Between 11 AM and 1 PM, they'll only cross once (at noon). For each remaining hour between 1 PM and 5 PM, the clock's hands will cross once. That gives us a total of 6 + 1 + 4 = 11 times.

What's Next?

The sequence is based on the expanding geometric figures. After each figure reaches the outside perimeter, it starts again at the center.

Trying Triangles

Thirty-five triangles.

Flipping Pairs

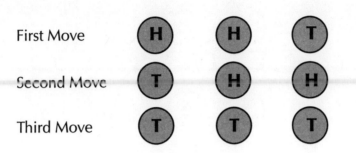

First Move	H	H	T
Second Move	T	H	H
Third Move	T	T	T

Missing Blocks

a. Twenty-three blocks. None are missing from the bottom layer, six are missing from the second layer, eight are missing from the third layer, and nine are missing from the top layer.

b. Seventeen blocks. Eight are hidden in the bottom layer, six are hidden in the second layer, three are hidden in the third layer, and none are hidden in the top layer.

Matchstick Memories

$$| = ||| - ||$$

$$| \times | = |$$

$$||| + | = |V$$

Sum Circle

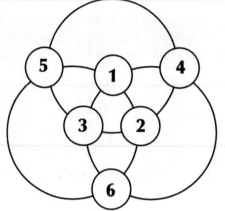

Many Rivers to Cross

First, the two children row to the far side. There, one gets out. The other child returns and gives the boat to an adult. The adult crosses the river. On the far side, the adult gets out and the child gets in the boat. The child brings the boat across the river and transports the other child back to the far side. This pattern continues until the four adults have crossed.

Train Travel

15 minutes and 32 seconds. This problem is not as simple as it may appear. The distance from pole one to pole ten is nine units. As stated, it takes the train 10 minutes to travel this distance. Therefore, it takes the train 1 minute and one-ninth (about 6.6 seconds) to travel each inter-pole distance.

From the first pole to the fifteenth pole is fourteen inter-pole distances. It should take 14 x 1 minute and 6.6 seconds, or 14 minutes and 92 seconds, or about 15 minutes and 32 seconds.

Miles Apart

120 miles. This problem is full of extra (and unneeded) information.

Think it backwards. One hour before they meet, one train is 65 miles away from the meeting point, while the other is 55 miles. Add the two distances together and you'll get 120 miles.

Passing Trains

792 feet. The length of the freight train can be calculated by knowing its relative passing speed and the time it took for it to move by. The passing speed is equal to the sum of both train speeds (60 mph +30 mph = 90 mph).

I lere's where some conversion comes in. By dividing by sixty, we find that 90 mph is equal to 1.5 miles per minute. By dividing by sixty again, we find that this is equivalent to 0.025 miles per second.

The freight train takes 6 seconds to pass. Therefore, its length is 0.15 miles. To change this into feet, multiply 0.15 by the number of feet in a mile (5,280).

Souped-Up Survey

The numbers do not add up correctly. The agency stated that only one hundred people were interviewed. Yet, according to a logical breakdown of the results, they received 120 responses. You can see this by making a diagram of the data.

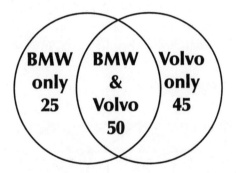

Toasty

Fry one side of two slices for 30 seconds. Flip one slice over and re-place the other slice with a fresh slice of bread. At the end of 1 minute, remove the completely fried bread. Return the unfried side of the previous slice to the pan and flip the other slice over for 30 seconds.

Circle Game

When added together, the numbers at the opposite ends of this sequence equal ten (1 + 9, 2 + 8, etc.). By placing a five in the middle circle, we ensure that all the sums must equal fifteen (10 + 5).

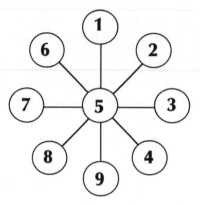

A Fare Split

$12.50. One-fourth of the total round trip fare ($5.00) was taken by Michelle alone. Three-fourths of the round trip was shared (half of $15.00). Therefore, Michelle should pay $5.00 + $7.50 or $12.50.

Pentagon Parts

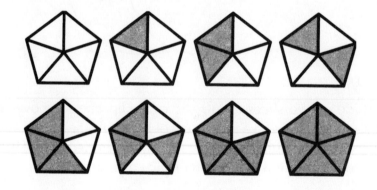

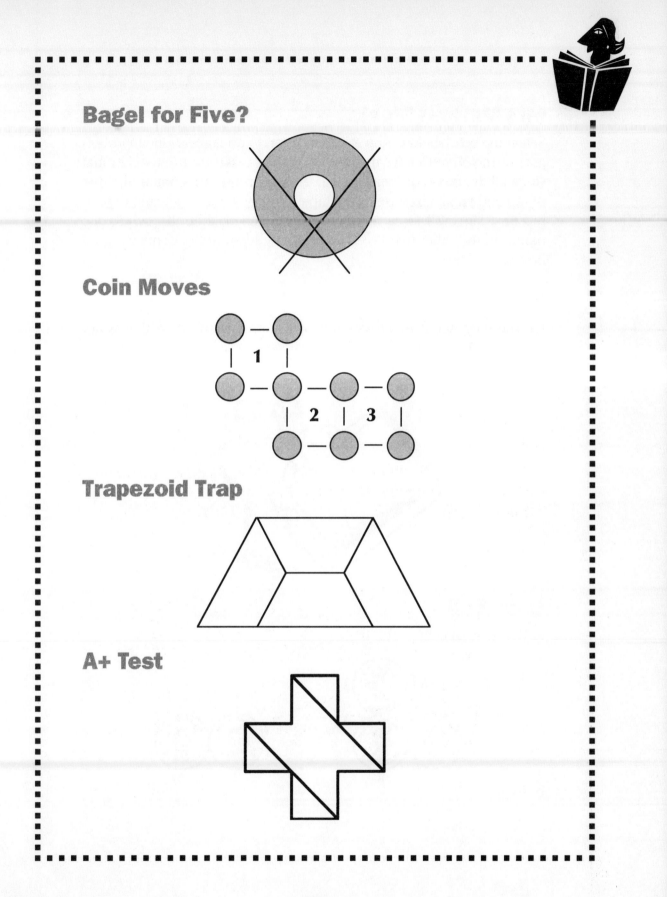

Bagel for Five?

Coin Moves

Trapezoid Trap

A+ Test

Mis-Marked Music

Select the box labeled "Rap & Jazz." Listen to one tape. If the marble is jazz, then you must have the box full of jazz cassettes. (Remember that since all the boxes are mislabeled, this box could not contain the mix of rap and jazz.) Likewise, if the tape is rap, you have selected the all-rap box. Since all three names are mismatched, then just switch the names of the other two boxes to correctly identify the contents of all boxes.

Measuring Mug

Fill the mug about two-thirds full of water. Then tilt it so that water pours off. When the level of water reaches the same height as the up-lifted mug bottom, the vessel is then half full.

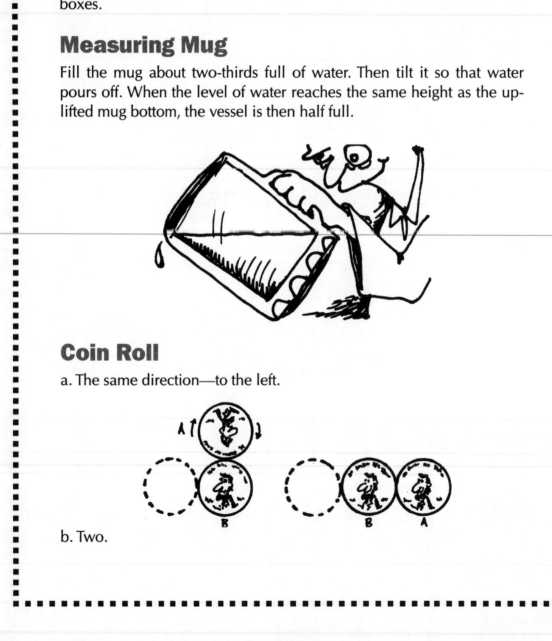

Coin Roll

a. The same direction—to the left.

b. Two.

Painting on the Side

Ten ways. 1 = all sides white, 1 = one red face, 1 = two adjacent red faces, 1 = two opposite sides red faces, 1 = three sides red (in line), 1 = three faces red (in right-hand and left-hand L-shape design), 1 = four faces red (in line), 1 = four faces red (two pairs of two in line), 1 = five red faces, 1 – all faces red.

Magic Triangle

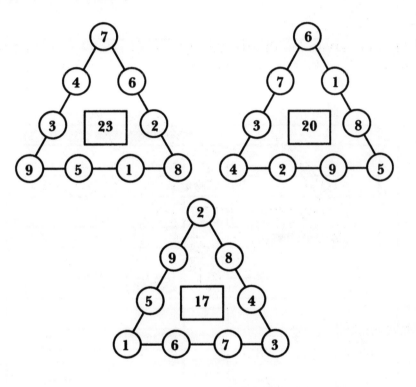

Patterns

Fourteen. Add the upper left number, lower left number, and lower right number together. Then multiply this sum by the number in the upper right corner. The product is in the center of the square.

Frog Jump

Four days. During the first day, the frog jumps up 6 feet and at night slides down 2 feet. The frog begins day two at a height of 4 feet, jumps to 10 feet, but slides back to 8 feet. On day three, the frog jumps to 14 feet, but slides back to 12 feet. On day four, the frog jumps to 18 feet and leaves the well.

Army Ants

Yes. Here's how.

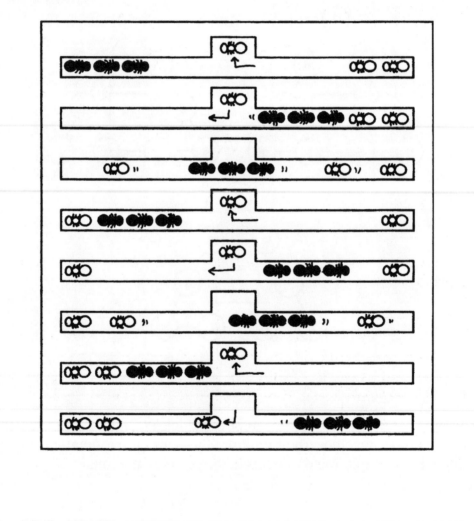

No Sweat

Five girls and two boys. First, subtract the coach's 9 cups from the total amount. Therefore, the boys and the girls together drank 34 cups. The winning combination is five girls (who together drink 20 cups) and two boys (who together drink 14 cups). 20 + 14 = 34 cups.

Go Figure!

Statement 4. The confusing relationship may best be understood by putting the information in a graphic layout. From the drawing, you can see that only statement 4 is true.

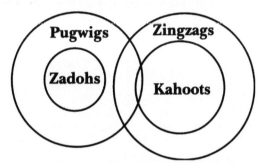

Square Pattern

There are only three distinguishing patterns. All other patterns are obtained by rotating the square.

r	g	b
b	r	g
g	b	r

b	g	r
r	b	g
g	r	b

g	r	b
b	g	r
r	b	g

Bouncing Ball

Approximately 3 meters. The first fall is 1 meter. It rebounds to ½ meter, than falls ½ meter. So now we're at 2 meters. Then the ball goes up and down ¼ meter, then ⅛ meter, then ¹⁄₁₆ meter, and so on. It continues this pattern until it comes to rest (theoretically it would keep going, but in the real world it stops). If we were to add all of these distances up, we'd get: $1 + ½ + ½ + ¼ + ¼ + ⅛ + ⅛ + ¹⁄₁₆ + ¹⁄₁₆ + ... = {\sim}3$ meters.

Complete the Pattern

X = 22; Y = 25. Each circle equals 1, each square equals 5, each triangle equals 10, and the pentagon equals 2. The numbers represent the sums of the values in each row or column.

Checkerboard

Thirty squares.

Cutting Edge

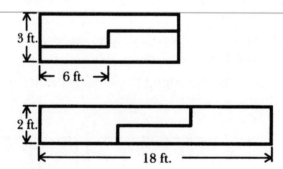

The Die Is Cast

Although all four dice have the same relative orientation of spots, the three spots on the last die tilt from the lower left corner to the upper right corner.

When the other dice are rotated onto this position, their three spots tilt from the upper left to the lower right corner.

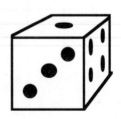

Playing with Matches?

Thirty-one matches. If one winner is to be found in thirty-two teams, then thirty-one teams must lose. Since each team can only lose once, the thirty-one losses result from thirty-one matches.

Competing Clicks

Anthony. The actual period is 1 second less than the time given. Emily completes ten clicks in 9 seconds. Buzzy completes twenty clicks in 19 seconds. Anthony completes five clicks in 4 seconds. This gives us the approximate rates: Emily = 1.1 clicks/second, Buzzy = 1.05 clicks/second, Anthony = 1.25 clicks/second.

Another Pattern

Four. The number in the center of each triangle results from dividing the product of the top two sides by the bottom side.

Vive le Flag

Twenty-four combinations. If both of the outside stripes are the same color, you'll have twelve possible combinations (4 x 3 =12).

If all three stripes are a different color, you'll have twenty-four possible combinations (4 x 3 x 2 = 24). However, these twenty-four flags are made up of twelve mirror-image pairs. Just rotate the mirror image one-half turn and you'll produce the other flag. This decreases the stripe combinations to only twelve.

Now let's add the two sets of possible combinations: 12 + 12 = 24 different color patterns.

Pizza Cut

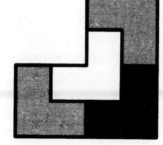

Slip Sliding

You'll get blocked if you don't place the coins in a specific order. Each coin must come to rest on the spot where the previous coin began its journey. Only in this manner can you then place all seven coins.

A, B, See?

10	55	919	545
x10	+55	+191	+455
100	110	1110	1000

Spare Change

$1.19. Jonathan has four pennies, four dimes, one quarter, one half dollar. Added together, they amount to $1.19.

Puzzling Prices

Ten dollars. The trick is not getting fooled into thinking that the book is five dollars.

If the book is "p," then $5 + ½p = p.

$5 = ½p.

$10 = p.

Gum Drop

135 gum drops. If forty gum drops are left in the jar, the forty must represent two-thirds of the gum drops that were available when Britt appeared.

Therefore, the total number of gum drops before Britt took her share was sixty. Working with the same logic, you can figure out that before Tanya took her share of thirty, the jar had ninety gum drops. Before Michael took his share of forty-five, it had 135 gum drops.

Go-Cart Crossing

33.3 minutes. To travel 1 mile, go-cart A takes ⅙ of an hour, go-cart B takes ¹⁄₁₂ of an hour, and go-cart C takes ¹⁄₁₅ of an hour. To travel one loop distance (⅓ of a mile), it would take each ¹⁄₁₈, ¹⁄₃₆, and ¹⁄₄₅ of an hour, respectively. All three would meet at ⅑ of an hour intervals. For five meetings to occur, five ⅑ hour periods must pass. 5 x ⅑ = ⁵⁄₉ of an hour, or about 33.3 minutes.

Table Manners

Two ways. White = female. Black = male.

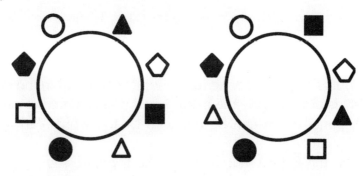

Winning Slip

The contestant picks one of the slips. The slip is placed out of view (possibly eaten). The contestant then asks the MC to read the slip that was not selected. That MC's slip has the word "loser." When the audience hears "loser," they logically conclude that the contestant must have picked the winning slip.

Ancient Man

60 years old. If his whole life is "X years," then:
His boyhood years = ¼X
His youth = ⅕X
His adulthood = ⅓X
His elder years = 13
¼X + ⅕X + ⅓X + 13 = X
X = 60

Lights Out!

He covers the window as shown here, which meets both conditions.

Pencil Puzzle

V. The layout is based on the sequence of letters found in the alphabet. The "twist" is produced by the extra pencil points aimed at certain letters. Each pencil point can be replaced by the words "advance one step."

Look at the letter L (either one). The L progresses to M. The M, however, does not advance to an N because two M pencil points converge on this next space. The letter then advances one extra step, resulting in an O.

With the same logic, the O leads to an R (advance three steps). The R leads to a V (advance four steps).

Sounds Logical?

Niko. If Sheila picks rock 'n' roll, then according to (1) Ramon must pick jazz and according to (2) Niko must also pick jazz. These selections contradict (3). This rules Sheila out.

If Ramon picks jazz, then according to (1) Sheila must pick rock 'n' roll and the same contradictions surface.

The only person who can select either jazz or rock 'n' roll without any contradictions is Niko.

Triangular Tower

Twenty balls arranged in four levels.

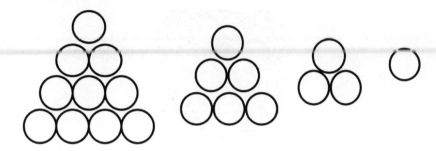

Criss-Crossed

Place one coin on top of the corner coin.

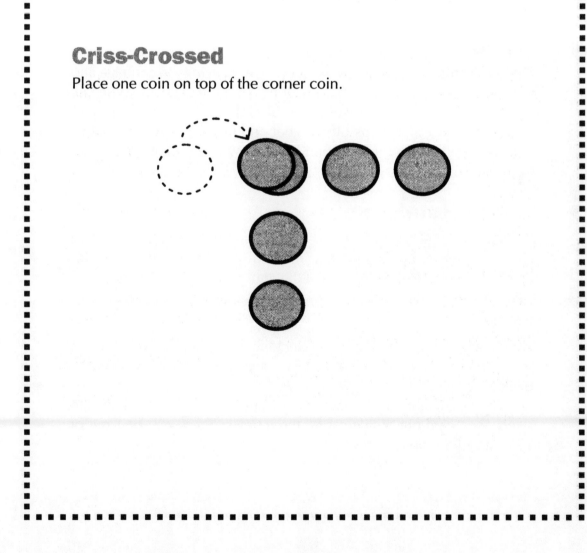

Crystal Building

Twelve tennis balls. Place six in a circle around the middle of the ball. Place three on top and three on the bottom.

Testy Target

Two arrows struck the 8 region (16 points) and seven of them struck the 12 region (84 points). Total: 16 + 84 = 100 points.

Eighth-Century Enigma

On his first trip, the man brings the goat over (leaving the cabbage and wolf behind). On his second trip, he brings over the cabbage. When he lands on the other side, however, he takes the goat back in his boat. When he returns, he drops off the goat and takes the wolf. He transports the wolf across the river and leaves it with the cabbage. He returns once more to ferry over the goat.

Planet Rotation

The sun would now appear to rise in the west and set in the east. This change is caused by the switch in rotation spin. The switch in revolution does not affect the direction of the apparent sunrise or sunset.

Shuffle

The straight is more probable. To select the four of a kind, you need to select "one card out of five cards" four times: $\frac{1}{5} \times \frac{1}{5} \times \frac{1}{5} \times \frac{1}{5}$, or 1 out of 625.

For the straight, the first card can be any card. Then, you'll need to select "one card out of five cards" three times: $\frac{1}{5} \times \frac{1}{5} \times \frac{1}{5}$, or 1 out of 125—a better probability.

Some Exchange

a. 14 and 9. The sum of all eight numbers is sixty. Each column must have a sum equal to half that, or thirty. To arrive at thirty, you need to lessen one column by five and increase the other by the same amount. This is accomplished by exchanging a 14 for a 9.

b. 2, 1, and 3. As with the previous problem, you can add all nine numbers together, then divide that sum by three.

The result is twenty:

7	2	1
3	6	2
10	**12**	**17**
20	**20**	**20**

Section 3
CHALLENGING
Critical Thinking
PUZZLES

Introduction

Data, data, and more data. We live in an age when the acquisition and presentation of new knowledge and information is astonishing. From the Internet to CD libraries, new technologies generate the means by which information transfer attains extraordinary dimension.

Since the access and acquisition of new knowledge continues to expand, we must learn to cope with this information overload. We need to develop and nurture thinking skills and strategies that will help us examine, evaluate, and apply new knowledge in a fair-minded manner. That's where critical thinking skills come in.

Although some educators and psychologists use the term "critical thinking" broadly by applying it to a range of thinking abilities, most restrict the use of it to specific strategies that help us better interpret and apply facts.

Educators and psychologists don't agree on the most effective way to develop these skills. Some feel that they should be taught independent of any content, such as real-life situations. This way the strategies are not confused or compromised with the importance of content. As a result, critical thinking skills can be more effectively considered as independent tools that can be applied to a range of circumstances.

Other experts, however, think that content is essential to teaching critical thinking skills. By utilizing real-life situations, students may then appreciate the value of these skills in the analysis of facts. This combination forms an intricate network of connections that produce a deeper understanding of content while offering a thinking platform from which to analyze additional situations.

It is with the latter approach in mind that this book was put together. As in the first two sections, this section uses challenging puzzles as an arena to practice critical thinking skills. So hang on to those brain cells as you tackle this final section.

—Michael

Puzzle Paths

Sam Loyd was one of the most published and brilliant puzzle creators of all time. Born in 1841, Sam was an accomplished chess player by his early teens. He created puzzles based upon the moves of chess pieces. Loyd also produced thousands of other puzzles, many of which still appear today with contemporary twists and slight modifications. The maze below is based upon one of his earliest puzzle ideas. Can you complete the challenge?

The *Amusing Amusement Park* has three rides. It also has three gates with signs that identify the ride to which they lead. The only problem is that the architect forgot the layout of the connecting paths. Can you help? Draw three paths that connect the rides to their gates. The paths can't meet or cross.

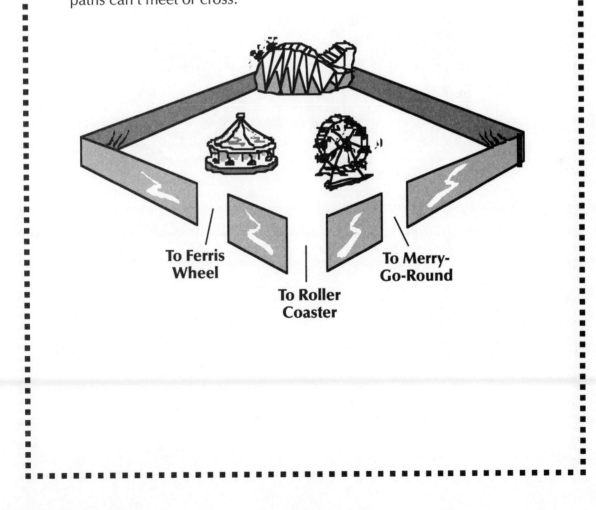

To Ferris Wheel

To Roller Coaster

To Merry-Go-Round

Turn, Turn, Turn

Ever heard of a multiaxial stimulator? Years ago, it appeared as a training device for astronauts and pilots. Nowadays, it's often found at beaches, amusement parks, and fairs. The MAS consists of three loops, each inside of the other. Each loop is free to rotate in only one dimension. The "pilot" is fastened to the middle of the innermost loop. In this position, a person gets to experience all three turning motions at the same time.

Let's strap the number "4" in this simulator. Suppose each of the loops made one half rotation. How would the "4" appear after it was flipped, turned, and spun halfway in all three dimensions? You can select from the choices below.

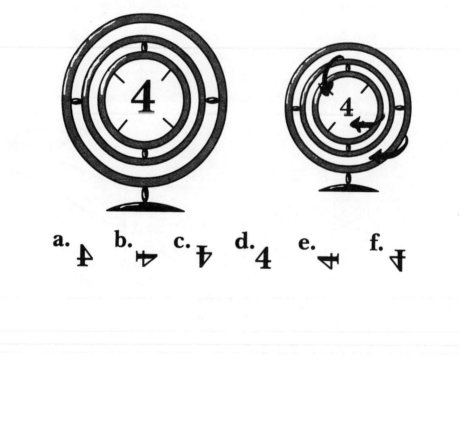

Mind Bend

According to Einstein, in some places the shortest distance between two points is not a straight line! Consider this: In space, the gravitational field of huge objects is strong enough to warp space. In these curved dimensions, the concept represented by a straight line bends to fit the framework of the distorted space. Mind bending, huh?

Here's another type of mind bender. The shape below is made from a single index card. No section of the card has been removed or taped back in place. Can you duplicate its appearance using several snips of a scissors? Have fun!

Whale of a Problem

In spite of their name, killer whales don't hunt and kill people. In fact, these dolphin-like animals prefer to eat smaller marine animals, such as seals and penguins. Biologists believe that rare attacks on humans occur because of misidentification. Obscured by daylight or icebergs, the image of a person may be mistaken for that of a penguin from below.

Now here's the problem. Acting alone, it takes two killer whales 2 minutes to catch two seals. Based upon this rate, how long will it take a pod of ten killer whales to catch ten seals?

Main Attraction

Like all magnets, a bar magnet has a North and South Pole. At each of these poles, the magnetic force is the strongest. It is powerful enough to attract and repel iron objects. Near the middle of the magnet, however, the force is hardly detectable.

Suppose you have two identical iron bars. Only one of the bars has been magnetized. Suppose you can only pick up and manipulate one bar of these two bars. How can you tell if it is the magnetized or unmagnetized bar?

Runaway Runway

"Good afternoon. This is your captain speaking. We're fourth in line for departure. As soon as these four albatross birds take off, we'll begin our flight. Thank you for your patience."

Strange, but true. Pilots must sometimes compete with birds for runway usage. The same physical principles that lift an aircraft into the sky are at work in our feathered friends. Runways that are constructed to offer better lifting conditions for aircraft inadvertently produce great takeoff locations for birds.

Speaking of runways, here's our puzzle. If an airport has three separate runways, there can be a maximum of three intersections. Suppose there are four runways. What is the maximum number of possible intersections?

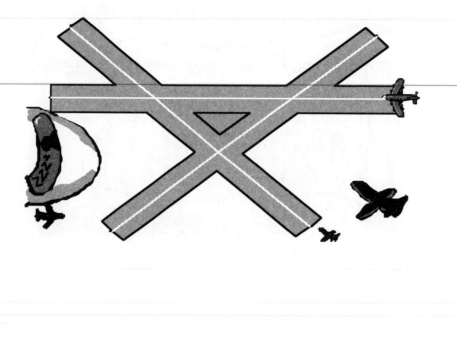

Raises and Cuts

Like many modern-day products, paper toweling arose from a factory mistake. A mill-sized roll of paper that should have been cut and packaged into soft bathroom tissue was manufactured thick and wrinkled. Instead of junking the roll, the workers perforated the unattractive paper into towel-sized sheets. And so, the paper towel was born.

Several years ago, Moe and Bo began work at a paper towel factory. At the end of the first week, the owner evaluated both workers. Pleased with Moe, she increased his weekly wage by 10%. Disappointed with Bo, she cut her salary by 10%. The following week, the owner decided to make their salaries more equal. To do so, she cut Moe's new salary by 10%. At the same time, she increased Bo's salary by 10%. Now, which worker earned more?

The Race Is On

The material we call rubber is another product of a mishap in the kitchen! Prior to the mid-1800s, rubber was a troublesome material. In the summer heat, it became soft and sticky. In the winter cold, it became hard and brittle. In searching for a way to improve the properties of rubber, Charles Goodyear accidentally spilled a spoonful of a rubber and sulfur mixture onto his stove. When he later examined the solidified spill, he discovered a flexible material that could withstand heat and cold.

Take a look at the two solid rubber wheels below. Both have been modified by retired ice skaters. On the first wheel, 4 pounds of lead are positioned in one central lump. On the second wheel, the same amount of lead is spread out into four 1-pound lumps so that they are positioned closer to the wheel's rim.

Suppose these wheels are released down identical inclines. If we don't consider air resistance, will these wheels accelerate at the same rate?

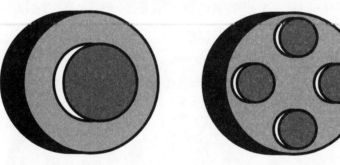

Screwy Stuff

Take a close look at the two screws below. Suppose they were both turned in a counterclockwise rotation. What will happen to each screw?

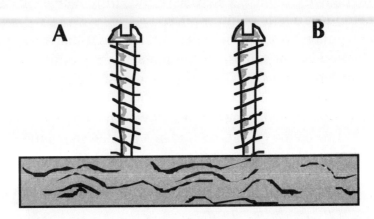

A   B

Screws in the Head

The pitch made by a vibrating string is dependent upon several factors, including the tension in the string. The more tightly pulled (greater tension), the higher the pitch. Likewise, if the string is relaxed (less tension), it produces a note of lower pitch.

Many guitars have a screw-like arrangement that varies the tension in the individual strings. As the tuner head is turned, this movement is transferred to a post. The turn of the post changes the tension in its wrapped string to produce a note of different pitch.

Take a look at the tuning heads below. What happens to the pitch of the sound when the head is rotated in a clockwise manner?

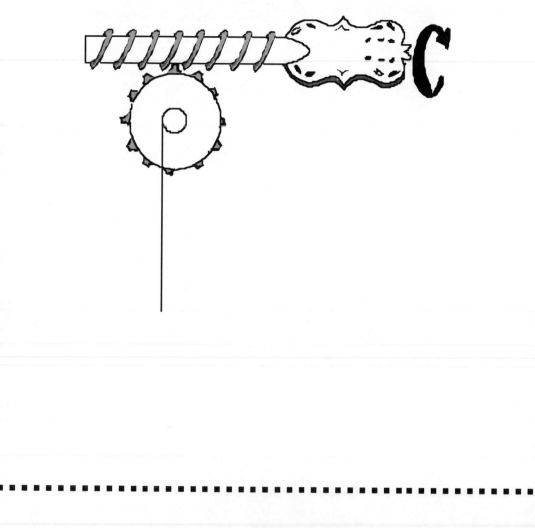

Change of Pace

Here are two puzzles that use a handful of change.

Consider this: I have ten coins in my pocket. The value of these coins is 50 cents. How many coins of each denomination are there?

Okay, so that one wasn't too difficult. How about finding the identity of thirty coins whose value is $1.00?

Spiral²

While exploring the ruins of an ancient city, an archaeologist uncovers an odd structure. The structure is made of stone walls that form a square spiral. The sides of the outside spiral measure 100 feet x 100 feet. The path throughout the entire structure is 2 feet wide.

If the archaeologist walks along the exact center of the path, how far will he travel from the entrance to the end of the spiral?

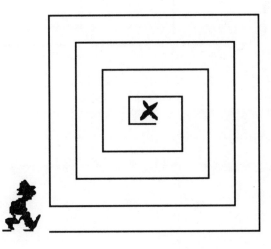

Take 'em Away

This arrangement of toothpicks forms fourteen different squares of various sizes. Can you remove six toothpicks and leave only three squares behind?

Don't Stop Now

Now that you are familiar with the pattern, let's try one more removal problem. Starting with the same twenty-four toothpick grid, remove eight toothpicks and leave exactly three squares behind.

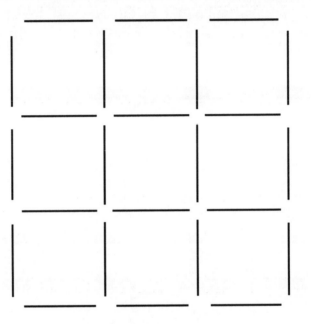

Get Set. Go!

Two cyclists race along a straight course. The faster of the pair maintains an average speed of 30 mph. The slower cyclist averages 25 miles per hour. When the race ends, the judges announce that the faster cyclist crossed the finish line one hour before the slower racer. How many miles long was the racing course?

Coin Roll

Run your fingernail around the rim of a dime or quarter and you'll feel a series of small ridges. These ridges appeared on coins hundreds of years ago. At that time, many coins were made out of silver and other valuable metals. To prevent people from "shaving" the metal from the edge of the coin (and selling the metal shavings), telltale ridges were added to the coin's rim. If a coin's edge was cut away, the telltale ridges would be lost.

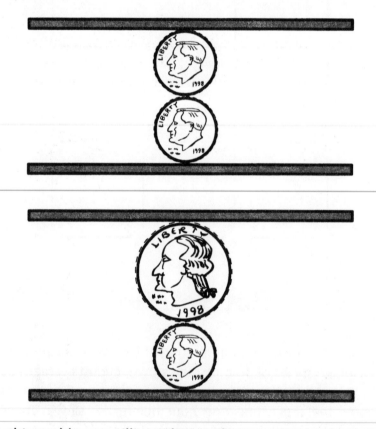

In this problem, we'll use those ridges to prevent the coins from slipping. Consider two dimes within a track formed by parallel chopsticks. Although the coins can move, their snug fit makes both coins move at the same time. Therefore, if we were to rotate one of the dimes,

the other would spin at the same speed but in the opposite direction. This results in both dimes moving along the track and maintaining their relative head-to-head position. Suppose, however, we change our setup and replace one of the dimes with a quarter. If the quarter is rotated along the track, how would its head-to-head position with the smaller dime change?

More Coinage

The four coins are positioned at the corners of a square. The side length of this square (measured from the center of each coin) is 8 inches. Here's the challenge. Can you change the positions of only two coins so that the new square formed by the coin arrangement has a side length slightly more than $5\frac{1}{2}$ inches?

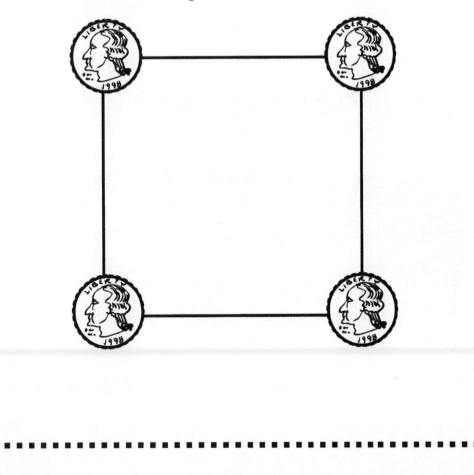

Some Things Never Change

People have written down puzzles for nearly 5000 years. One of the first puzzle collections was recorded about 1650 B.C. on a scroll called the Rhind papyrus. The word *Rhind* comes from the name Henry Rhind, a Scottish archaeologist who explored Egypt. *Papyrus* is a paper-like material that was used as a writing tablet by the ancient Egyptians.

The Rhind papyrus is a scroll that is over 18 feet long and about a foot wide. It was written on, on both sides, by a person named Ahmes. Roughly translated (and somewhat updated), one of the puzzles from the scroll is presented below.

There are seven houses, each containing seven cats. Each cat kills seven mice, and each mouse would have eaten seven ears of corn. Each ear of corn would have produced seven sacks of grain. What is the total number of all of these items?

Doing Wheelies

The outer rim of each "double wheel" is twice the diameter of the wheel's inner rim. Suppose the top wheel rotates at ten revolutions per second. At what speed will wheel A and wheel B spin?

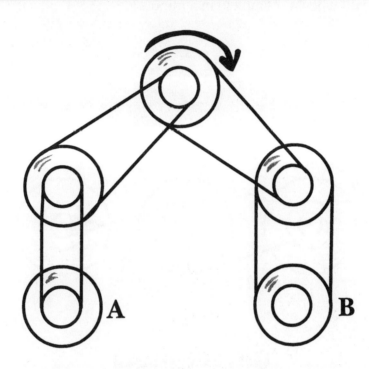

More Wheelies

The outermost rim of these wheels is twice the diameter of the middle rim. The middle rim is twice the diameter of the innermost rim. Suppose wheel A rotates at sixteen revolutions per second. How many revolutions will wheel C complete in a minute?

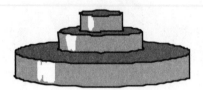

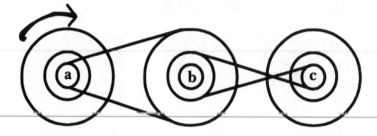

Good Guess

In order to win a free visit to the dentist, students had to guess the exact number of gumballs in a fish bowl. The students guessed 45, 41, 55, 50, and 43, but no one won. The guesses were off by 3, 7, 5, 7, and 2 (in no given order). From this information, determine the number of gumballs in the bowl.

Check It Out

The six sections below are parts of a 5 x 5 checkerboard grid. Can you piece them back together to form the original pattern?

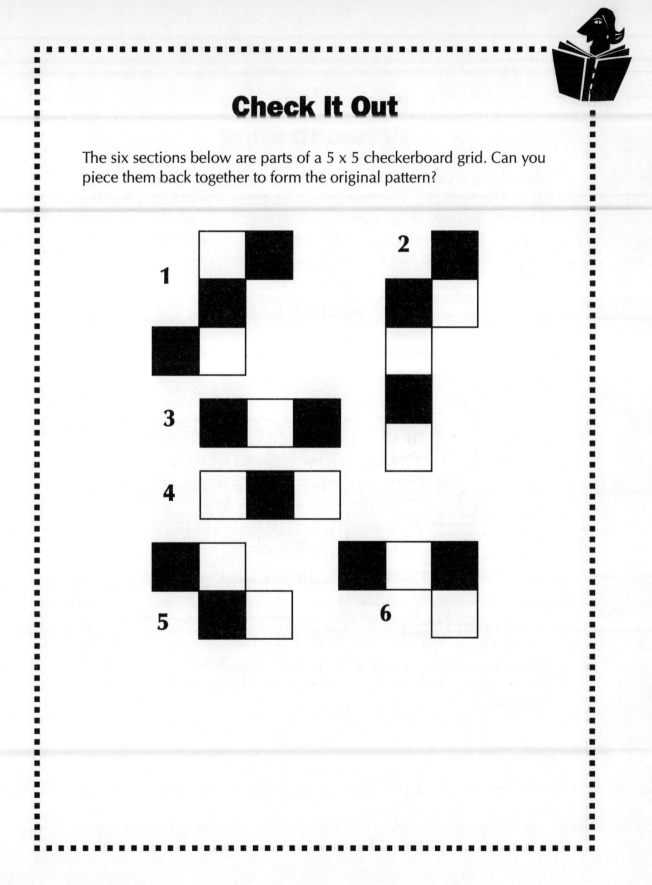

Oops, I Wasn't Concentrating

A pitcher is filled to the brim with grape juice. While raiding the refrigerator, Anthony accidentally knocks the pitcher over so that half of the contents spill out. Hoping no one will notice, Anthony adds tap water to the half-filled pitcher, bringing the volume of the diluted juice to the top. He then pours himself a glass of the watered down juice, leaving the pitcher three-fourths full.

"Yuck! This needs more flavor!" he exclaims and then adds more grape flavor by filling the pitcher to the brim with double-strength grape juice.

How does the concentration of this final solution compare with the original grape drink?

THAT TAKES CARE OF THE JUICE. NOW, TO FIND THE TAPE FOR THE BROKEN EGGS.

Trying Times

The triangle below is divided into four equal parts. Suppose you can paint one or more of these four smaller parts black. How many different and distinguishable patterns (including the pattern which has no painted triangles) can you form?

Remember, each pattern must be unique and not be duplicated by simply rotating the large figure.

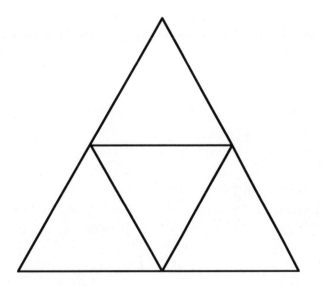

Bridge, Anyone?

Ever heard of Galloping Girdie? If not, perhaps you've seen an old science fiction movie that showed a clip of a large suspension bridge twisting apart and falling into the river below it. That was Galloping Girdie.

It spanned a large river in the state of Washington. Soon after it was constructed, people noticed that winds would cause the bridge to sway and shake. During one incident of heavy winds, the bridge shook so violently that it fell apart into the river below. Bye-bye, Girdie.

Now, it's your turn to design a bridge. To build it, you'll need three ice cream sticks. If you don't have these sticks, you can use three pieces of stiff cardboard. The cardboard sections should be 4½ inches long and ½ inch wide.

Position three cups in a triangular pattern. The cups should be placed so that the edge-to-edge distance between any two of the cups is 5 inches.

Hmm... 5-inch canyons, but only 4½-inch bridges. Your job is to construct a bridge using these three pieces and span the gaps connecting all three cups.

Face Lift

Take a look at the shape below. Although it is made up of four identical cubes, you can only see three of them. The fourth cube is hidden in the bottom backcorner. Imagine picking the shape up and examining it from all angles. How many different cube faces can you count?

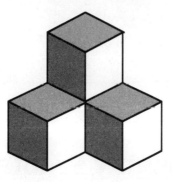

Okay, so it wasn't that hard. Try this one. The "double L" shape is made up of six cubes. The sixth cube is hidden in the back of the middle layer. If you could examine the stack from all angles, how many faces would you see?

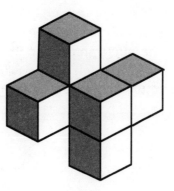

Okay, okay, okay. Here's one more. This one consists of only five cubes. Actually it resembles the "double L" shape, except that one of the cubes is removed.

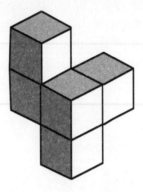

Weighty Problem

Did you know that during periods of weightlessness, astronauts lose bone mass? To prevent any serious loss, people in space must exercise. Stressing and stretching body parts help keep bone material from being reabsorbed into the body.

For a moment, let's imagine our weightless astronaut returning to Earth. She steps onto a scale and weighs herself. When the lab assistant asks her for her weight, she offers an obscure (but challenging) answer.

"According to this scale, I weigh 60 pounds plus half my weight."

Can you figure out how much this puzzling space traveler weighs?

Number Blocks

Take a look at the three stacks of numbered blocks below. Can you re-arrange the blocks by exchanging one (and *only* one) from each of the three stacks so that the sum of the numbers in each stack is equal to the sum of numbers in either other stack?

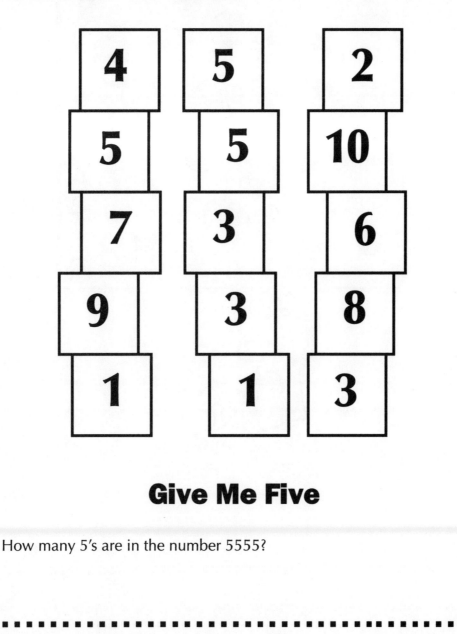

Give Me Five

How many 5's are in the number 5555?

Separation Anxiety

Using three straight lines, separate the apples from the oranges.

Breaking Up Is Hard to Do... Sometimes

Take a look at the square and triangle below. Both figures are divided into four equal and identical parts so that each part has the same shape of the original figure (only smaller).

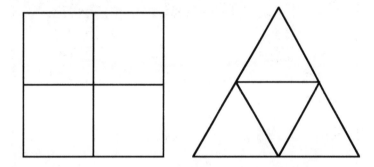

So far, so good. Now try to divide the figure below into four equal and identical parts, each with the same shape as the original figure.

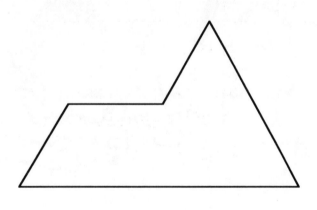

195

Mind Slice

Close your eyes and imagine a perfect sphere. Now, imagine a cleaver placed at a point anywhere on the surface of the sphere. How does changing the angle of the cleaver slice affect the *shape* of the exposed faces?

Say Cheese

The total surface area of any cube is equal to the sum of the surface areas of each of the six sides. For example, the cheese cube below measures 2 inches on each side. Therefore, the surface area of each side equals 2 inches x 2 inches, or 4 square inches. Since there are six sides, the total surface area of this cube is 24 square inches.

Now, the challenge. Using as many cuts as needed, divide this cube into pieces whose surface area sum is *twice* the surface area of this 2 x 2 cube.

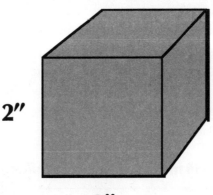

2"

2"

Satellite Surveyor

Satellites that orbit the Earth can see all sorts of things. Spy satellites, for example, have lenses that are powerful enough to "read" license plate numbers on cars. Other types of satellites can "look beneath" the Earth's surface. Some of these images have been used to uncover lost civilizations that have been buried for thousands of years under shifting desert sands.

In this problem, we'll use our satellite to help survey a plot of land.

The basic plot is a square that measures 20 miles on a side. Suppose the midpoint of each side is used as a marker to divide the entire plot into nine plots of various sizes and shapes. Without performing any higher math magic (just stick to plain ol' logic, with a little geometry), what is the area of the shaded central square?

NOTE: Before you bask in premature glory, it is not equal to 100 square miles!

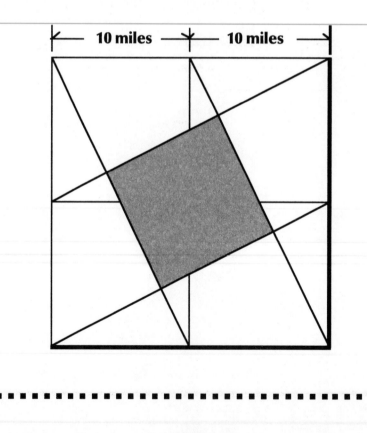

Magic Star

For those of you who are tired of magic squares and magic triangles, may we present *The Magic Star?* In this puzzle, you'll have to use the numbers one through twelve. Only one number can be placed in a circle, and all the numbers must be used. When placed correctly, the sum of all rows of four must be the same.

HINT: All of the side sums equal twenty-six.

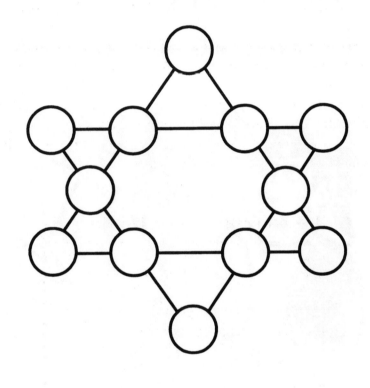

Keep on Tickin'

Divide the face of a watch into three sections. The sum of the numbers included on each section must equal the sum of the numbers on either of the other two sections. Let's not waste any time—the clock is ticking.

Cards, Anyone?

Use a pair of scissors to carefully cut out two unequal corners of an index card as shown below. Can you now use the scissors to cut this modified card into two identical halves?

　　NOTE: The identical halves must be formed without flipping either piece over.

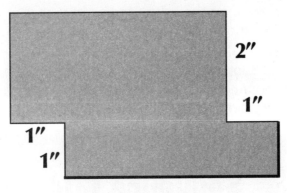

　　Let's keep up the cutting challenge. Copy the pattern below onto an index card. Use your scissors to trim off the excess card stock. Now, here's the challenge. Divide this shape into four equal and identical parts that can fit back together to form a perfect square.

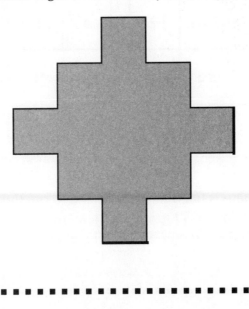

Going Batty

Click, click, click, click. Like submarines, bats have a sonar system called echolocation. They use their echolocation to find objects. The clicking sounds made by bats move outward like the beam of a light-house. When the sounds strike an object (such as an insect meal), they are reflected back to the bat's large ears. With incredible speed, the bat's brain analyzes the echo return time and uses it to accurately lo-cate the target's position.

Now, let's put that echolocation to work. Over a five-night period, a bat targets and captures a total of a hundred beetles. During each night, the bat captured six more beetles than on the previous night. How many beetles did the bat catch on each night?

Sequence Grid

A sequence grid is formed by items that are related by their order. Here are two examples. As you can see, the placement of the numbers and letters reflects a sequence.

512	256	128
64	32	16
8	4	2

A	C	E
G	I	K
M	O	Q

The first square is filled in an order based on dividing a number in half. The second square illustrates a sequence of letters that is sepa-rated by single (but not recorded) middle letters.

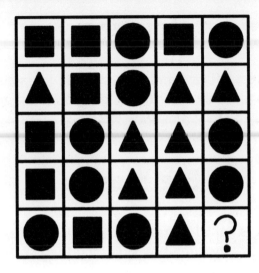

Now that you know what a sequence grid is, here's one to sharpen your puzzling skills on.

Breaking the Rules

A ruler is placed on two pieces of chalk as shown below. As the ruler is pushed, it moves 4 inches ahead. How far did either one of the chalk pieces roll?

Balance

Suppose you have a balance and a 2-gram and 5-gram mass. How can the balance be used only three times to separate 80 grams of fat into piles of 13 grams and 67 grams?

Big Magic

The figure below is called a magic square. Do you see why it's called magic? The sum of any three-box side (and the two three-box diagonals) is equal to the sum of any other side (or diagonal). In this case, they are all equal to fifteen.

8	3	4
1	5	9
6	7	2

The sections belong to a four-by-four magic square. Your job is to assemble these sections into a complete sixteen-box magic square. To do so, you'll *first* have to uncover the sum of the side for this figure.

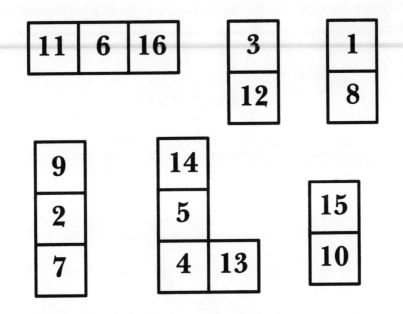

Togetherness

A computer and its monitor weigh a total of 48 pounds. If the monitor weighs twice as much as the computer, how much does each piece of hardware weigh?

Look Over Here

Note the direction in which each eye looks. Can you uncover the pattern? Good. Now find the empty eye. In which direction should this eye be looking?

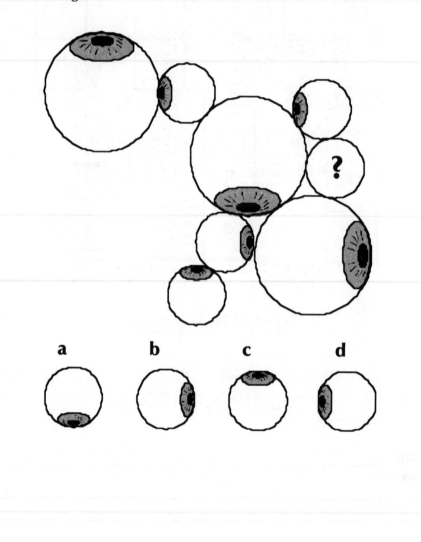

a   b   c   d

Time on Your Hands

Examine the series of three clockfaces shown below. When you uncover the pattern of the hand movement, select from the choice of times the one that will be closest to what the fourth clock should read.

7:07 4:07 7:22 4:22 7:15 4:15

Take Your Pick

Arrange eight toothpicks (on a flat surface) so that they form two squares and four triangles.

One Way Only

Can you trace the following figure using only one continuous line? Place your pencil anywhere on the figure. Then, draw the rest of the figure without lifting your pencil from the page.

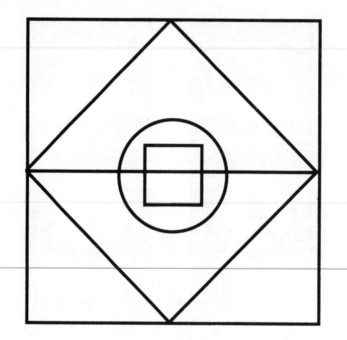

NOTE: This line cannot cross over itself nor retrace any part of its path.

Lasagna Cut

A square pan filled with piping-hot lasagna is set aside to cool. When the hungry chefs return, they discover that a quarter of the lasagna has mysteriously disappeared (as shown below). Frustrated, they decide to divide the remaining piece into four equal portions before any more is eaten. All cuts must be normal—no slicing through the plane of the surface allowed. What is the cutting pattern that will meet the needs of these chefs?

    HINT: The simplest solution requires cutting this meal into eight pieces and supplying each person with two smaller pieces.

Iron Horse Race

Two trains race against each other on parallel tracks. *The Casey Jones Special* is a coal-fed steam engine that travels at a respectable speed. The newer, oil-burning *Metropolitan Diesel* travels 1½ times the speed of *The Casey Jones Special*. To make the race a closer competition, *The Casey Jones Special* begins the race 1½ hours before its opponent. How long will it take the *Metropolitan Diesel* to catch up to the slower steam engine?

Thick As a Brick

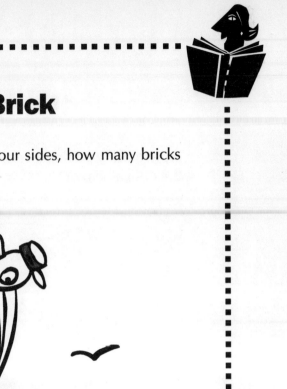

If the chimney below is complete on all four sides, how many bricks does the whole structure contain?

Here, Art, Art, Art

How quickly can you uncover the perfect five-pointed star hidden in the design below?

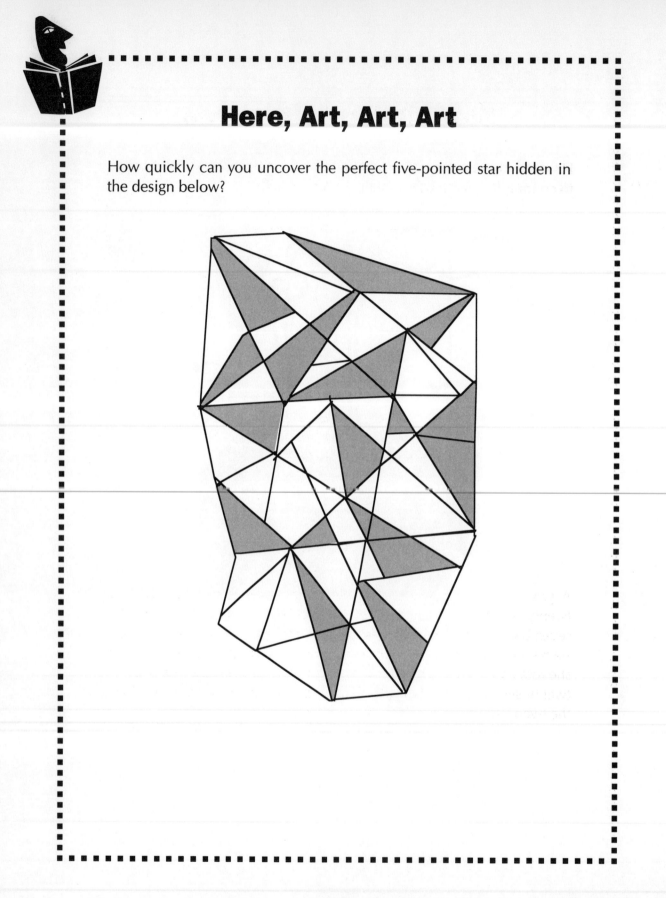

Surrounded by Squares

How many squares can you uncover in the pattern below? Don't forget to count the outer border as one of your answers!

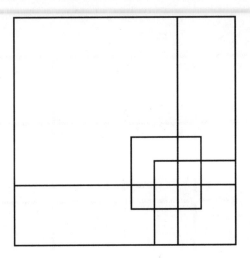

More Cheese

A grocer has a large cube of cheese that she wishes to divide into twenty-seven smaller and equal-sized cubes. To cut out the twenty-seven blocks, she uses two cuts to divide the cube into three slices. She stacks these slices atop of each other and makes two more cuts. Finally, she rotates the cube a quarter-turn and makes the final cut. The result is twenty-seven identical cubes made with six cuts. Is it possible to get the twenty-seven cubes with fewer cuts? If so, how?

Break It Up!

If you look carefully, you'll be able to uncover thirty squares in the toothpick pattern below. Your challenge is to find the fewest number of toothpicks that, when removed, leaves no complete square pattern intact.

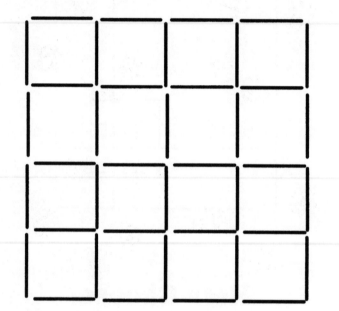

Exactly... Well, Almost

Which of the designs below is unlike the other five?

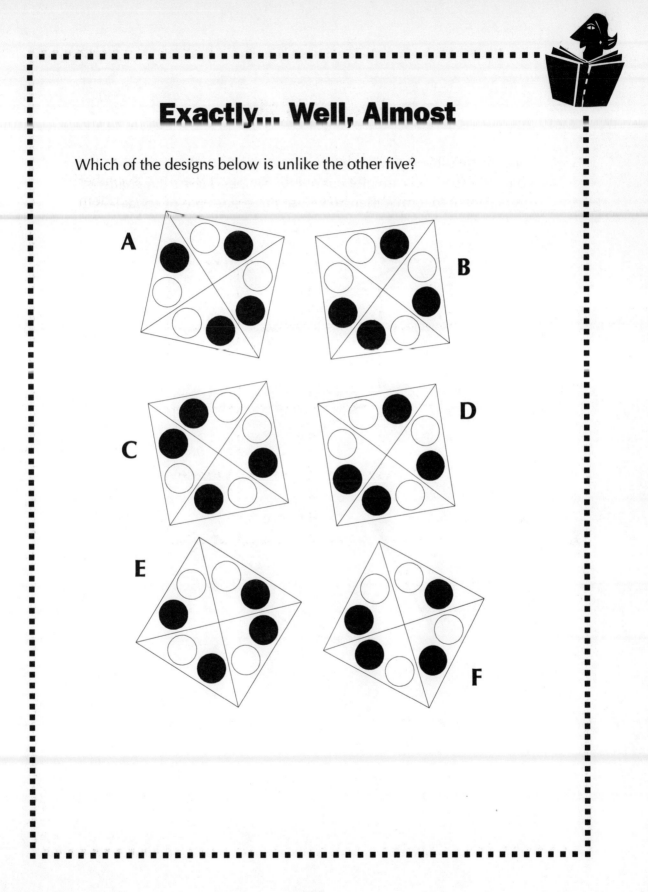

Parts of a Whole

Copy the five shapes shown below onto a separate sheet of paper. Use a pair of scissors to carefully cut out the shapes. Here's the challenge. Arrange them to form a triangle whose three sides are of equal length.

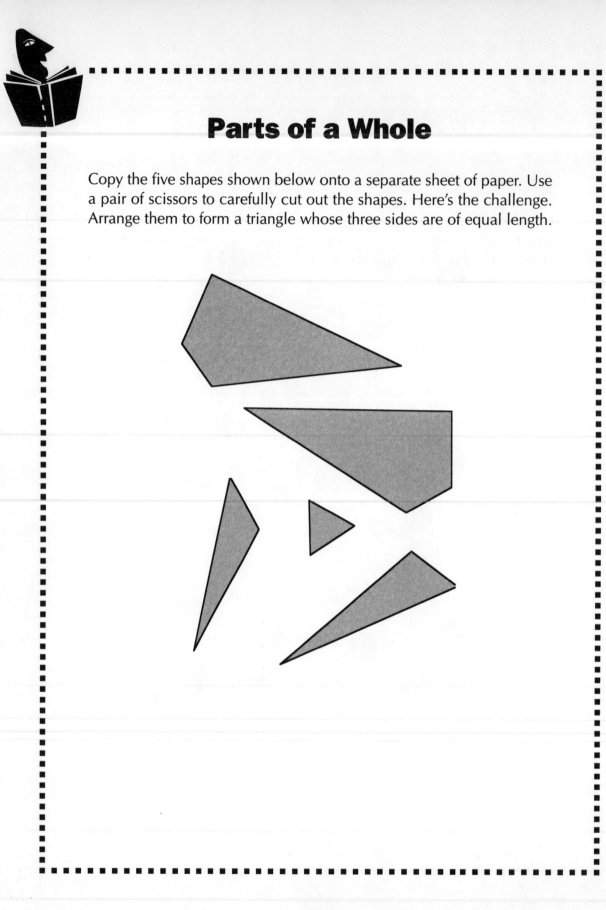

A Game for Losers

The object of this modified game of tic-tac-toe is to lose! In order to win, you must force your opponent to complete three squares in a row. Let's enter a game that has already been started. You are "O" and it is your turn. In which box or boxes should you place your "O" marker to ensure that you win by losing (no matter where your opponent goes)?

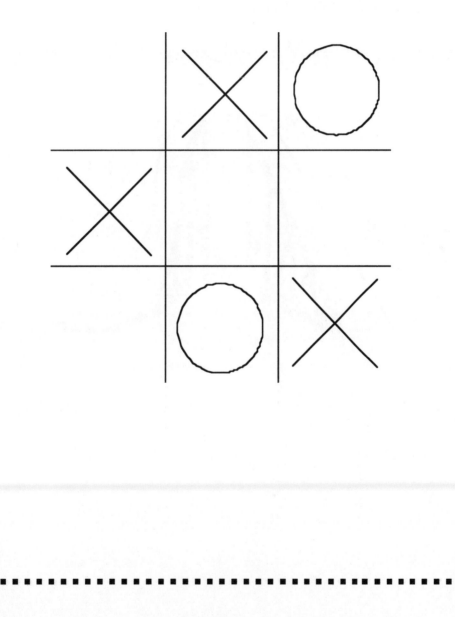

Roller Coaster, Roll!

Ed and his identical twin brother Ed build roller coaster tracks. They've just completed two hills that are both 40 feet high. As you can see, the slopes of the two hills are somewhat different. Ed (the older twin) rides a car that will travel along on a straight slope. Ed (the younger twin) rides a car that will travel along a curved slope.

If both cars are released at the exact same time, which Ed will arrive at the bottom of his slope first?

Sum Puzzle

Copy the pattern and numbers shown below onto a sheet of paper. Then carefully use a pair of scissors to separate the sheet into nine separate squares. Rebuild the larger square using the following strategy. The sum of any two adjacent numbers must equal ten. Have fun.

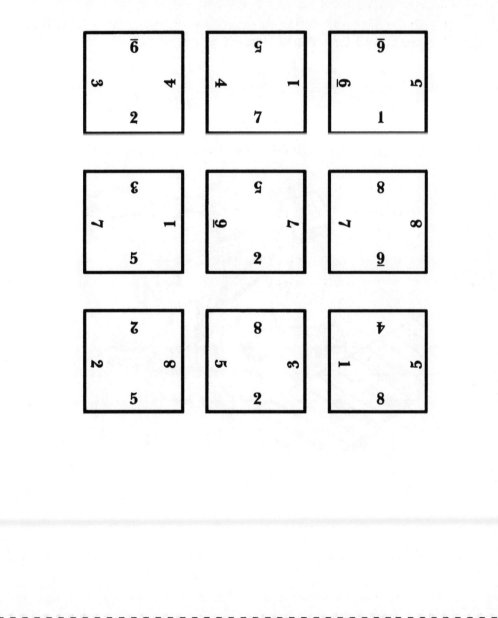

A Class Act

There are thirty students in a class. Five of these students do not play any sort of musical instrument. Among the others, eighteen students play guitar. Six of these guitar players also play keyboards. How many of the students in the class play only keyboards?

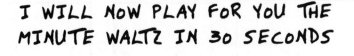

Cool Cut

Shut your eyes and try to imagine a perfect ice cube. If you're good at visualizing, you may be able to "see" the edges and faces that are positioned on the far side of the cube. Good. Now, here's the challenge.

With one cut, how can you divide this cube so that a perfect triangular face is exposed? Don't forget, a perfect triangle has all three sides of equal length.

WATCH IT. YOUR IMAGINATION IS LEAKING ONTO THE TABLE.

Melt Down

Unlike most liquids, water freezes into a solid that is less dense than its former liquid state. Since it is less dense, ice floats in water. At the surface, the ice acts as an insulator to help trap heat within the water below. This layer of frozen insulation actually insulates lakes, rivers, ponds, and oceans from freezing into a complete solid.

Now let's bring this information back to the kitchen. An ice cube floats freely in a glass filled to the brim with water. Will the water level rise or sink as the ice cube melts?

What's the Angle?

An equilateral triangle has three sides that are all of equal length. This familiar shape can be constructed from three identical pieces. Examine the shapes below. Which of these shapes illustrates this building block? Once you've selected the shape, make three copies of it on a separate sheet of paper. Cut out and arrange these pieces so that they form an equilateral triangle.

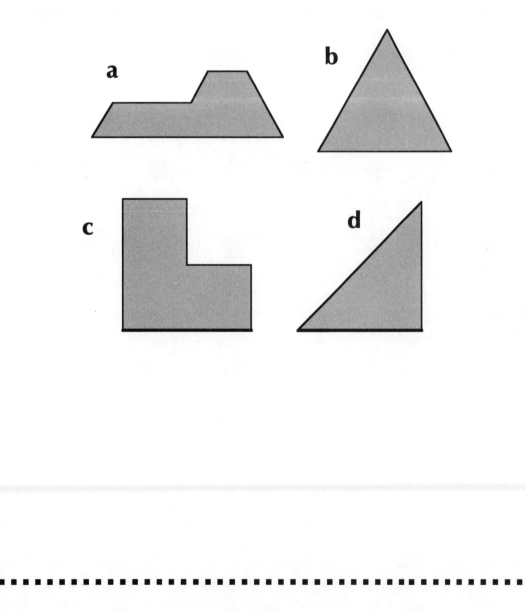

Here, Spot, Spot, Spot

Without lifting your pencil from the paper, draw six straight lines that connect all sixteen of the dots below. To make things more of a challenge, the line pattern that you create must begin at the "x".

Keeping Time

The strike of a lightning bolt can create a tremendous surge of electricity. If this electric flow reaches the delicate circuits of a computer, it can "burn out" the sensitive components. To prevent against this damage, computers are plugged into surge protectors, which stop the electric flow if a damaging level of electricity is detected.

In this problem, there are no surge protectors. Two electronic clocks are plugged directly into the wall socket. A surge of electricity flows through both clocks and affects their time-keeping circuits. One clock is now 5 minutes per hour fast. The other clock is now 5 minutes per hour slow. In how many hours will the clocks be exactly one hour apart?

225

Wrap It Up

You will soon engage your intellect in this book's final critical thinking puzzle.

Did you know that fortune cookies didn't originate in China? They were created in the U.S. by the owner of an Asian restaurant who wished to amuse his customers while they waited for their meals to be cooked. Over time, fortune cookies evolved into a treat that is now offered at the end of the meal. That's a wrap. And speaking of wraps...

Take a look at the steps in which the cookie wrapper below was folded. In the final step, two holes were punched through the layers of the folds.

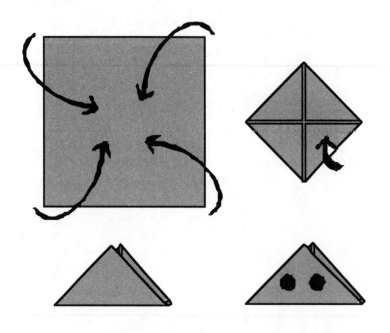

Now unroll this wrapper. Which of the patterns would it resemble?

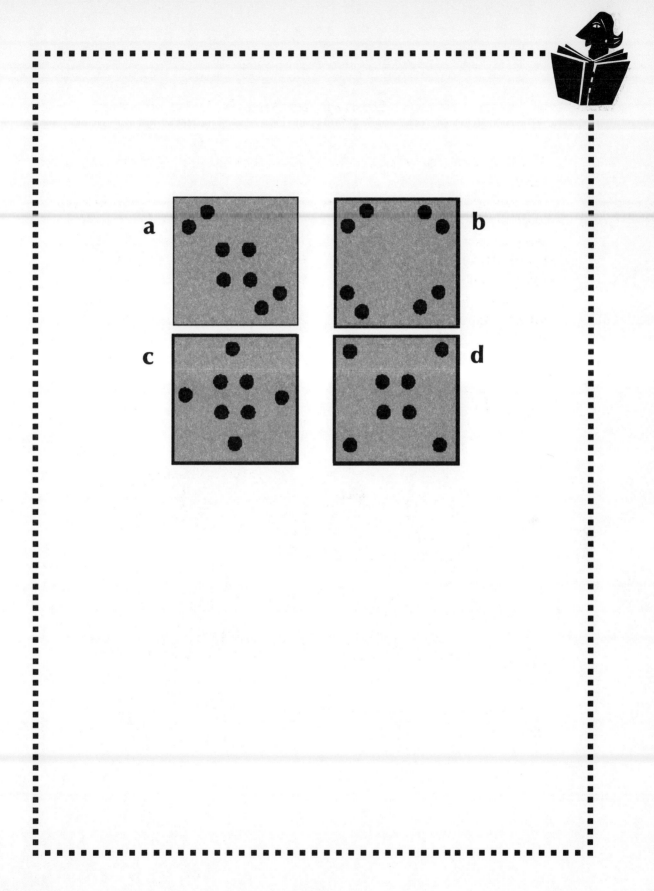

ANSWERS

Balance

First, use the balance to divide the 80 grams into two piles of 40 grams. Then divide one of the 40-gram piles in half. Now balance the 20 grams against the 7 grams produced by the two masses. The 13 grams that are removed from the balance form one pile. The 7 grams added to the 40 grams + 20 grams produces the larger pile of 67 grams.

Big Magic

The sum of the side is thirty-four, and the square looks like this:

1	11	6	16
8	14	3	9
15	5	12	2
10	4	13	7

Break It Up!

Nine toothpicks need to be removed as shown below.

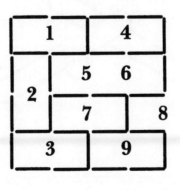

Breaking the Rules

Two inches. Each chalk piece will advance only half the distance covered by the ruler.

Breaking Up Is Hard to Do...
Sometimes

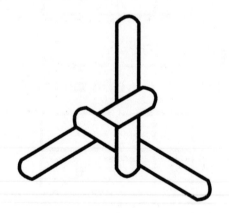

Bridge, Anyone?

The sticks below are arranged so that they support each other in a central triangle formed by overlapping and underlapping supports.

Cards, Anyone?

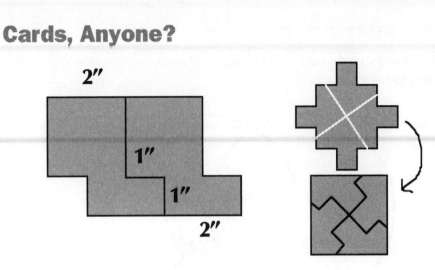

Change of Pace

a. either 5 pennies ($.05) + 4 nickels ($.20) + 1 quarter ($.25) = $.50; or 10 nickels ($.05) = $.50

b. 25 pennies ($.25) + 1 nickel ($.05) + 2 dimes ($.20) + 2 quarters ($.50) = $1.00

Check It Out

A Class Act

Seven students play only keyboards. A diagram helps illustrate and solve this problem.

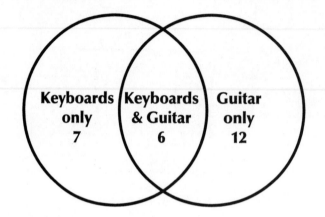

Coin Roll

The coins maintain their relative position to each other as they move along the track. What changes is the direction in which the coin images point.

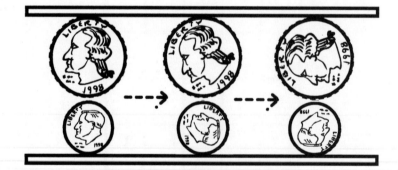

Cool Cut

Make the cut from one corner straight across to the corners as shown below. Each side of this regular triangle that is formed is equal in length to the diagonal of the square.

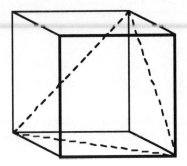

Doing Wheelies

Wheel A would be spinning at five revolutions per minute. Wheel B would be spinning at twenty revolutions per minute. The difference in speed results from the "gearing up" and the "gearing down" from the first wheel set to the second wheel set. The belts between the second and third wheel sets do not affect the spin.

Don't Stop Now

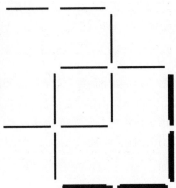

Exactly... Well, Almost

E. It is the mirror image of the other repeating (but rotating) design.

Face Lift

a. Eighteen faces.
b. Twenty-six faces.
c. Twenty-two faces.

A Game for Losers

By placing your "O" marker in either of the boxes indicated below, you are ensured a victory no matter where your opponent places his or her "X"s.

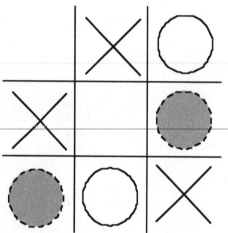

Get Set. Go!

150 miles long. In order to complete 30 miles of distance, the faster cyclist requires 1 hour of time while the slower cyclist needs 1.20 hours. Therefore, the time difference per 30 miles of travel is .20 hours. In order to increase the difference to 1 hour, multiple the 30 miles by 5.

Give Me Five

1111. Easy, unless of course you forget all it takes to solve this problem is to divide 5555 by 5!

Going Batty

The number of beetles captured on each successive night were 8, 14, 20, 26, and 32.

Good Guess

Forty-eight gumballs. Since two guesses were off by seven and no guesses were repeated, these values had to refer to numbers at the opposite extremes of the spread. The two extremes are 41 and 55. If you add 7 to one and take 7 away from the other, you arrive at the middle number of 48.

Here, Art, Art, Art

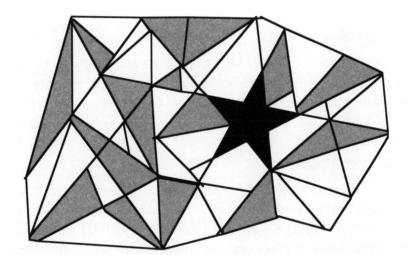

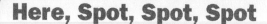

Here, Spot, Spot, Spot

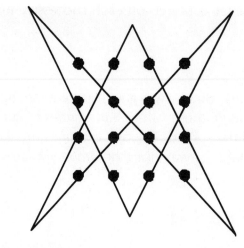

Iron Horse Race

The trains will be tied 3 hours after the faster train (or $4\frac{1}{2}$ hours after the slower train) begins the race. For example, if the trains travel 60 mph and 90 mph, the $4\frac{1}{2}$-hour journey for the slower train covers 270 miles, while the 3-hour journey for the faster train also covers 270 miles.

Keep On Tickin'

First you'll need to find out what each section needs to add to. To get this number, add up every number on the clock's face ($1 + 2 + 3 + 4 + 5 + 6 + 7 + 8 + 9 + 10 + 11 + 12 = 78$). Divide 78 by 3 and you'll get 26—the sum that each section must add to. The next part is relatively easy, since the numbers are already laid out in a ready-to-add pattern.

Keeping Time

Six hours. In 6 hours, the slow clock will be exactly 30 minutes behind while the fast clock will be exactly 30 minutes ahead of time.

Lasagna Cut

Each person gets one large and one small triangular piece.

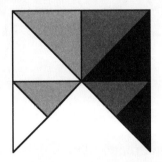

Here's a slightly different pattern that produces four similarly shaped slices (if we assume the connecting points between the triangle pairs remain uncut).

Look Over Here

b The direction of the look is based upon the number of neighboring eyes that are in contact with the eye's circumference. Eyes that "touch" three other circles (such as the circle in question) have a pupil that points to the right.

Magic Star

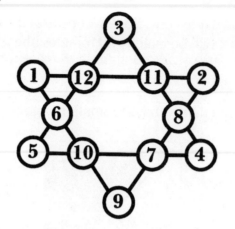

Main Attraction

Take either bar (it doesn't matter which one) and touch one end of the bar to the middle of the other bar. If the bar you are holding is a magnet, then its pole will cause the nonmagnetized bar to move. If, however, you've picked up the nonmagnetized bar, no attraction will occur. That's because neither of the poles is being touched.

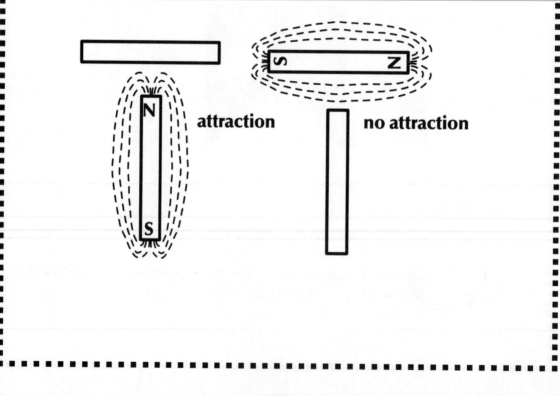

Melt Down

The level of water will not change. Although the top of the cube floats above the surface of the water, the amount of water in the entire ice cube can fill a space equal to the dimensions occupied by the part of the cube that is under the water's surface. In other words, as the ice cube turns to water, it produces the same amount of water as the space occupied by the submerged part of the cube.

Mind Bend

Place three parallel cuts in the card. Two of the cuts should be positioned on one side, while a single central cut should be made on the opposite side (as shown below). Then place a twist in the card so that half of the upper surface is formed by the "bottom-side" of the card. For extra fun, you might want to tape the folded card by all of its edges to the desk (making it more difficult to uncover the baffling "twist").

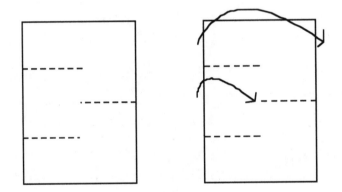

More Cheese

No. Six cuts are the fewest number of cuts needed to produce the twenty-seven smaller cubes. Stacking doesn't result in fewer cuts. Think of it this way: that innermost cube of the twenty-seven must be formed by a cut on each of its six sides.

Mind Slice

The angle of the cut will not affect the shape at all. All cuts will produce faces that are perfect circles. The feature that does change with the cutting angle is the circle size.

More Coinage

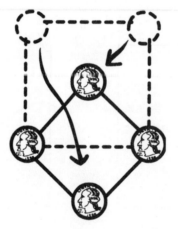

More Wheelies

480 revolutions. Since wheel B's rim is four times longer than wheel A's rim, it spins at one-fourth the speed (4 rps). Likewise, wheel B's rim is twice as long as wheel C's rim. Therefore, wheel C's rim spins twice as fast (8 rps). In 1 minute, C wheel will complete 60 x 8 revolutions, or 480 revolutions.

Number Blocks

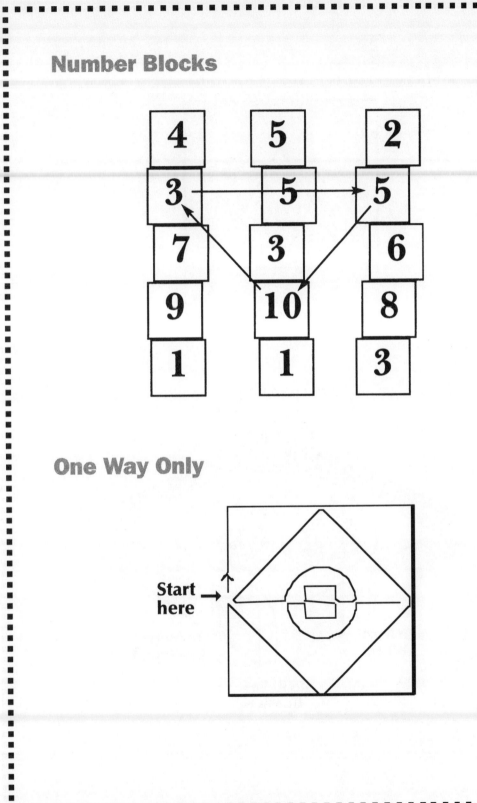

One Way Only

Start here →

Parts of a Whole

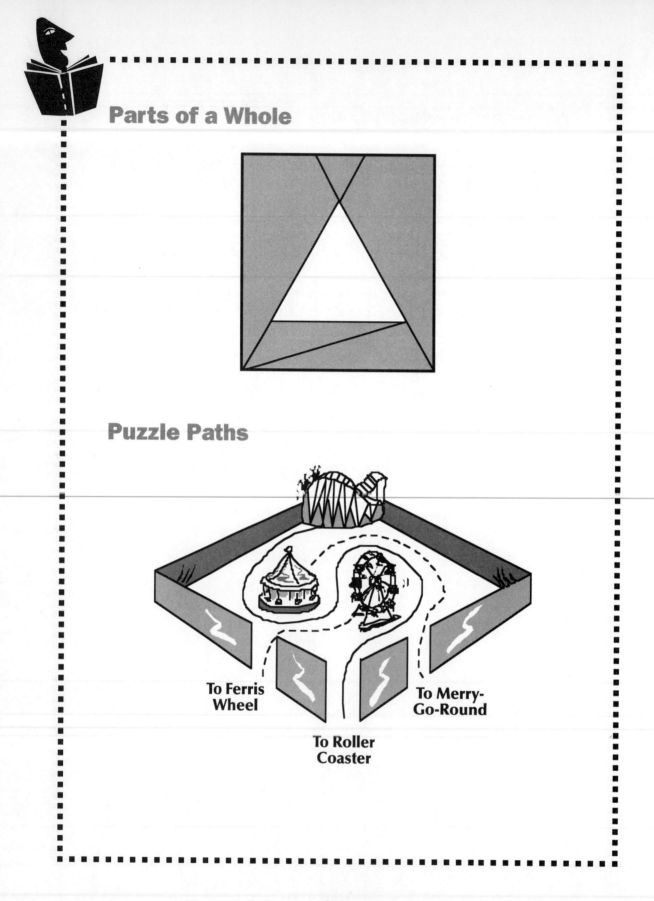

Puzzle Paths

To Ferris
Wheel

To Roller
Coaster

To Merry-
Go-Round

Oops, I Wasn't Concentrating

It is weaker than the original solution. In order to have the original concentration, Anthony would have to add grape juice that is 2½ times the regular strength.

Raises and Cuts

They are now both earning the exact same amount. To prove this, let's take a sample first-week salary of $100 for both Moe and Bo. After the first adjustment, Moe earned $110 while Bo earned $90. During the second adjustment, Moe was cut by $11 to $99. At the same time, Bo was increased by $9 to $99.

Runaway Runway

Six intersections as shown below.

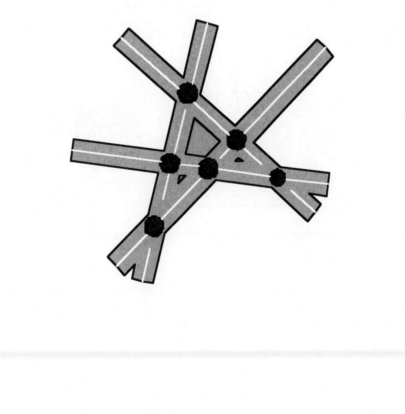

Roller Coaster, Roll!

Young Ed. The car that travels along the curved slope accelerates faster. This extra speed results from the quick drop in the path that allows the car to quickly pick up speed as the car moving down the straight slope accelerates at a slower and more uniform rate.

Satellite Surveyor

80 square miles. If you examine the dissected grid, you'll uncover that the composite shapes include side-by-side pairs that can be joined to form four squares. The total area is 20 x 20, or 400 square miles. Each of the five identical squares contains one-fifth, or 80 square miles.

Say Cheese

Make three cuts that divide the cube into eight smaller but equal cubes. Each of these eight cubes has a side length of 1 inch to produce a surface area of 6 square inches. The sum of the eight cube surface areas is 48 square inches.

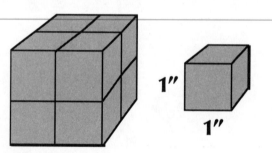

Screws in the Head

As the threads turn, they will produce a counterclockwise motion in the gear of the tuning post. This motion will decrease the tension in the string to produce a note of lower pitch.

Screwy Stuff

The threads of screw A form a spiral that would "go into" the wood block. In contrast, the opposite spiral of screw B would result in this screw moving out of the wooden block.

Separation Anxiety

Sequence Grid

Triangle. The grid is filled by a series of number sequences. The first sequence consists of only one member—a square. The second and adjoining sequence includes a square + circle. The third sequence expands to include a square + circle + triangle. The complete sequence from which the "?" can be determined is square + circle + triangle + triangle + circle + circle.

Some Things Never Change

$7 + 49 + 343 + 2401 + 16{,}807 = 19{,}607$.

Spiral^2

The complete path from entrance to center is 5000 feet. To obtain this distance, determine the total area of the structure (10,000 square feet). Now mentally unroll the spiral. Divide the 10,000-square-foot area by the area associated with one foot of forward travel. Since the corridor is 2 feet wide, the area for a single foot of forward motion is 2 square feet. Dividing 10,000 by 2, we arrive at the total distance of 5000 feet.

The Race Is On

The wheel with the centrally placed lead will accelerate fastest. This behavior reflects a property of physics that ice skaters execute during their moves. As a skater spins, the speed of the spin can be adjusted by altering his or her distribution of weight. As the arms extend, the spinning skater slows. As the arms draw in, the spin accelerates.

Sum Puzzle

Surrounded by Squares

Thirteen squares.

Take 'em Away

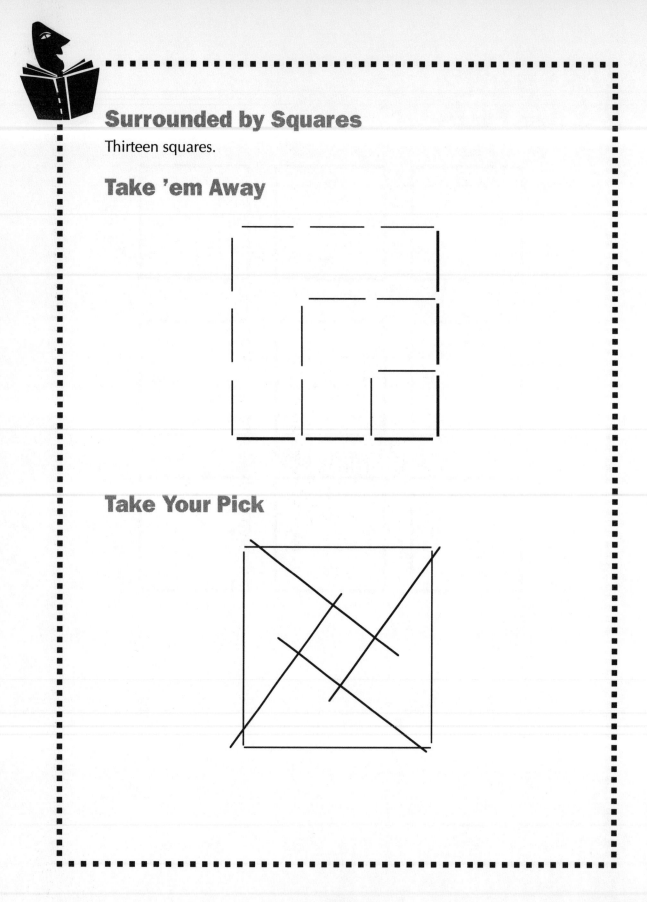

Take Your Pick

248

Thick As a Brick

Sixty bricks. You don't have to count all of the bricks. Just count the bricks in the uppermost layer (twelve) and multiply by the number of layers (five) so that you arrive at a total number of sixty bricks.

Time on Your Hands

7:22. For each given time, the minute hand advances a quarter of a complete counterclockwise rotation, while the hour hand advances three-eighths of a complete counterclockwise rotation. The final arrangement looks like this:

Togetherness

The computer weighs 16 pounds and its monitor weighs 32 pounds.

Trying Times

Eight unique triangles as shown below.

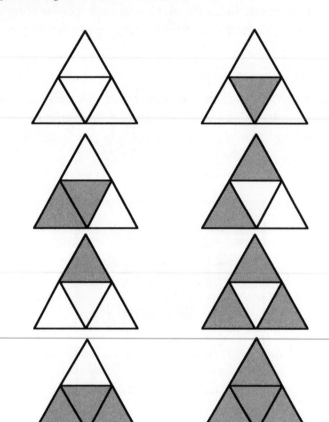

Turn, Turn, Turn

F.

Weighty Problem

120 pounds. If she needs to add "half of her weight" to get her full weight, then the weight that she does tell (60 pounds) must be half of her total. Therefore, 60 pounds is half of her weight. 60 + 60 = 120 pounds. If this doesn't seem right, just work it backwards starting with the 120 pounds.

What's the Angle?

a. Three copies of this shape are positioned as shown here.

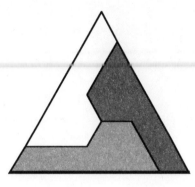

Whale of a Problem

Two minutes. The amount of time needed to catch the seals doesn't change. Since two whales can catch two seals in 2 minutes, it is logical to assume that a single whale can catch one seal in that same period of time. Likewise, three whales can catch three seals in 2 minutes. As long as the number of whales is equal to the number of seals, the time doesn't change. Therefore, ten killer whales will also take 2 minutes to catch ten seals.

Wrap It Up

d. Here's what you see as you unwrap the folds.

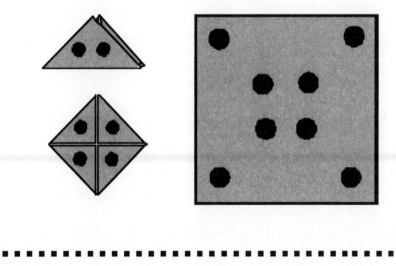

Section 4
Visual Thinking PUZZLES

Introduction

Visual thinking is a powerful element that defines the way in which we process all sorts of information.

Visual thinking isn't stuck in the present. We can use it to reflect back into the past. For example, think of when you first saw this puzzle book displayed on the shelf of a bookstore. Was it on an upper or lower shelf? Was it standing alone or was it part of a stack? Now imagine when someone first placed this book on the shelf. Think back even further to when another person delivered a box of these books to the bookstore. Perhaps you might even be able to think back to what might have been going on when the author was writing this introduction. That's the power of visual reflection.

Visual thinking can just as easily jump into the future. Think of a domino balanced upright on a desktop. Now, in your mind's eye place five other dominos close to this one so that a row is formed. Now, push against the first domino until it falls over. What happens as it strikes the next domino? Do all the dominos fall? What happens when the final domino tumbles? Do any of them fall off the table? Again it's that power of visual thinking that allows you to "fast forward" into the future.

This book contains a collection of puzzles that have been developed, tweaked, and twisted into mindbending challenges that are sure to test your visual thinking skills. Many of the puzzles are based upon traditional challenges that have been around for hundreds of years. Others are brand new. But instead of me telling you about these eye-brain busters, why not experience them yourself? Open your eyes and mind and have fun!

—*Michael*

Wrap It Up

You don't need a crystal ball to see into the future. All you need is your brain.

The shape below is formed from three smaller pieces. These pieces are connected by a tiny hinge at their point of attachment. Suppose you were able to rotate the pieces so that neighboring sides aligned flatly and squarely. Which one of the shapes below could this structure look like?

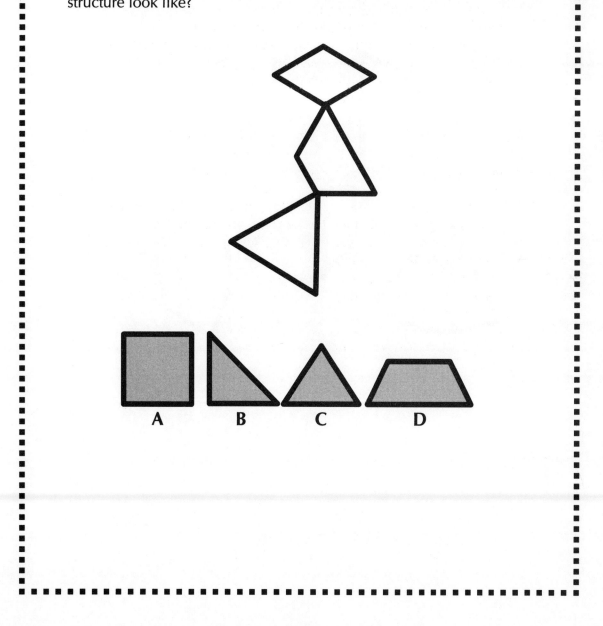

A   B   C   D

Pi Pieces

There are many skills we associate with visual thinking. Some of these skills may be much more difficult to master than others. For example, the ability to mentally rotate objects is often harder than we might imagine.

Try this: If you were to assemble these pieces into a circle, what would the figure formed by the inner lines look like?

Connect the Dots

Here's a different type of puzzle. To solve it, your brain must uncover patterns.

How many squares can you create in this figure by connecting any four dots?

Note: The corners of the square must lie upon a grid dot.

Pizza Pi Problem

Think about pizza. Imagine its sauce-and-cheese covered surface. Not too hard to do, is it? This ability to produce "images" within our brain is a product of visual thinking. Now, let's get back to pizza.

Bob likes to prepare personal pizzas. He begins with a circle of dough that is 12 inches in diameter. On top of the dough, he places slices of salami. All of the slices are round and have a 4-inch diameter. If Bob doesn't overlap the slices or allow any of the slices to extend beyond the edge of the pie, what is the maximum number of salami slices he can add?

Point the Way

There are all sorts of patterns. Here's one that is based upon a sequence in which some sort of change occurs over time.

Can you uncover how this sequence of tiles changes? If so, use what you've visualized to identify the fourth member of this series.

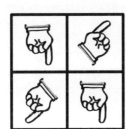 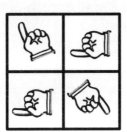 

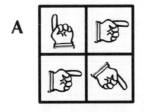

A

B

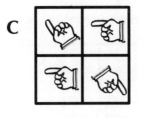

C

D

Mirror Madness

Do you realize that your brain is constantly trying to make sense of the information sent to it by your eyes? You may already know that the image that falls upon the retina of the eye is upside-down. Your brain, however, flips the image over into a more logical upright appearance. Perhaps your brain can flip images "on cue?"

"Mirror, mirror, on the wall, which of the choices below is the reflection of the following tile?"

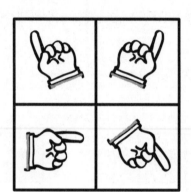

A    **B**

C 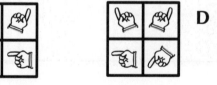 **D**

Spacing Out

For a moment, let's leave the eye-brain puzzles and just "space out."

A shuttle astronaut leaves her craft to work on a disabled satellite. She lands on one corner of the satellite (which is a perfect cube) and realizes that she must walk across the satellite's surface to the opposite corner. To conserve oxygen, she must follow the shortest possible route. Is her planned route (identified by the dotted line) the shortest path between opposite corners?

Code Caper

What animal is represented in the code below?

Hint: From our earliest years, we learn to identify objects by the space they occupy. Artists, however, sometimes use the space that doesn't occupy something. It's called negative space and it's the fabric that surrounds things. Perhaps, a little negative space might help you solve this puzzle?

Link Latch

Your optic nerve links the eye and the brain. This "connecting wire" is not passive. As messages travel along its path, visual information is analyzed and sorted. By the time they arrive at the brain, the messages have already been partially processed and analyzed so that no time is wasted.

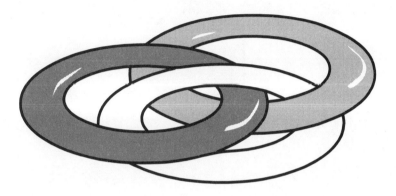

While digging through a box of links, a jeweler uncovers the three joined links shown above. She decides to separate the links. As she examines them, she finds a way to disconnect all three by opening just a single link. Can you?

Cut the Cube

Can you visualize 3-D space? If so, imagine a solid block of clay shaped into a perfect cube. Can you visualize it? Great. Now, let's change it with a modeling knife. How can a single cut produce the six-sided face shown here?

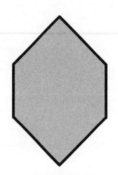

Square Deal

To solve this next puzzle, you'll need both visual thinking skills and a bit of eye-hand coordination (you'll also need a pair of scissors).

Trace the sections below onto a sheet of heavy-stock paper. Carefully cut them out with the scissors. Then arrange the pieces so they form a perfect square.

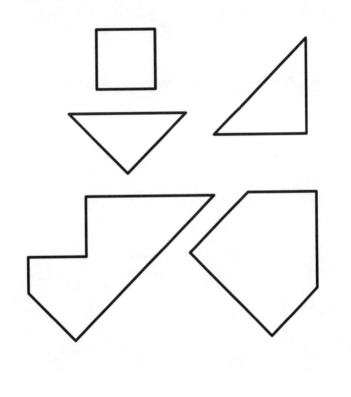

Reflecting Back

Imagine the hands of a standard clock in the position that indicates the time of 4:20. Suppose you looked at that clock in a mirror. Which of the following clock faces would the reflected image resemble?

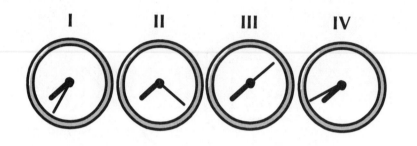

Okay, let's make it a bit more challenging. Suppose that the hands of a clock indicate the time of 2:40. Suppose you turned the clock upside down and then looked at its mirror reflection. Which one of the faces below would the reflected image resemble?

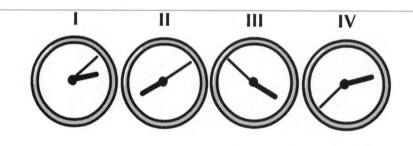

Naughty Notes

And now a musical distraction . . . Which pair of notes is unlike the other six pairs?

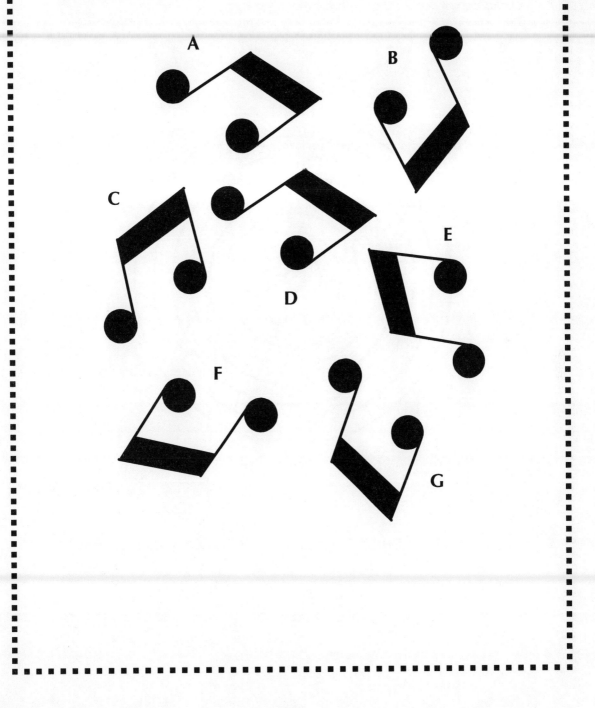

Amaze in String

A pipe is located at the center of an odd loop of string.
Suppose the string is pulled by its two free ends. Will the string come free of the pipe or will it be caught by it?

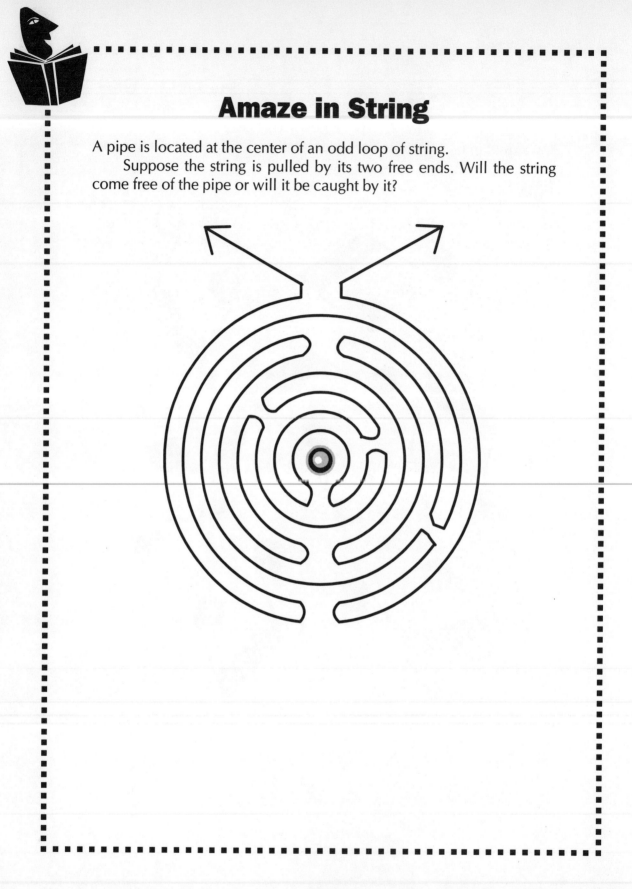

Broken Record

A phonograph record falls to the floor and splits into two equal halves. Suppose that the halves are carefully glued back together so that all of the grooves align. There is, however, a slight problem. In the rush to repair the album, the incorrect sides are paired. Therefore, each side of the record is a composite formed by half of side A and half of side B. Now let's set this record on a turntable and place a phonograph needle at the end of the first song. As the record spins will the needle:

     a) trace out a circle, always remaining the same distance from the center spindle?

     b) spiral in towards the center spindle (its normal motion)?

     c) spiral out towards the album edge?

This Side Up

Make four copies of this arrow pattern. Cut out each arrow along its outline. Then arrange the copies so that they form five arrows.

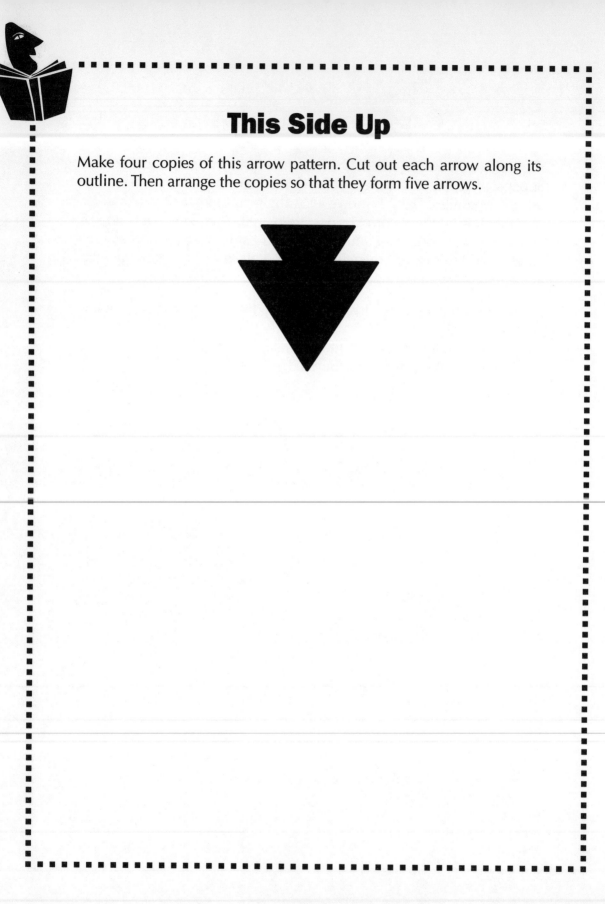

Prefab 4

Suppose the following pattern was folded up or folded back to form a house. Which one of the structures below could *not* be formed from this pattern?

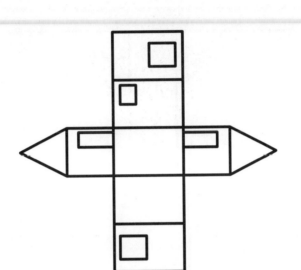

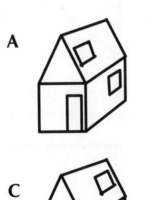

A

B

C

D

Superimposing Position

Suppose the values illustrated by the two graph forms below are added together. Which of the four choices will the combined final graph form look like?

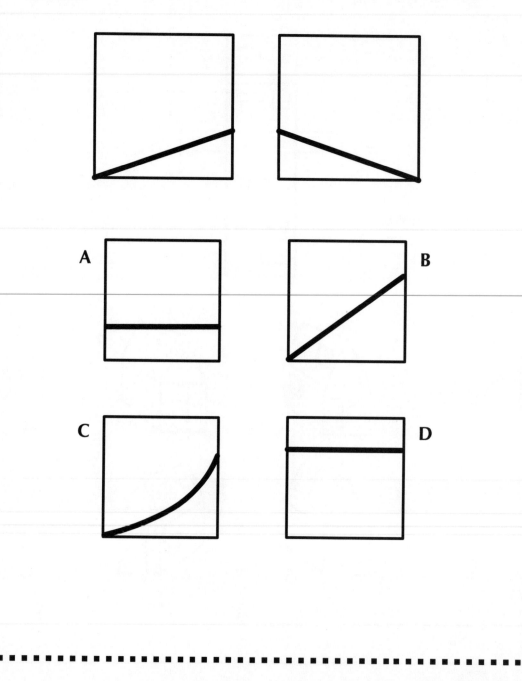

Hidden in Plane Site

Can you uncover fifteen squares outlined in the pattern below?

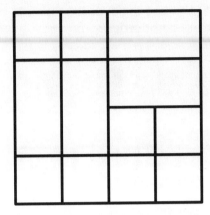

What Sign Are You?

The mathematical signs connecting the numbers below have been left out. Good thing we've supplied them on four tiles. Your job is to place the tiles between the numbers so that the final answer is 3. All operations are done in a left-to-right order.

$$\boxed{+} \quad \boxed{-} \quad \boxed{\times} \quad \boxed{\div}$$

Tying the Knot

As these two lovers slurp up a shared piece of spaghetti, will a knot form in the pasta (or only in their hearts)?

Pentagon Pieces

Trace these two pairs of shapes onto a sheet of heavy-stock paper. Use a pair of scissors to carefully cut out all four pieces. Then rearrange the shapes into a regular pentagon.

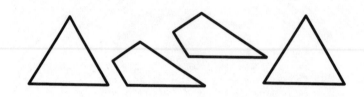

Pencil Stack

Which is the third pencil up from the bottom of the stack?

Boxed In

Which one of the following designs cannot be folded into a cube?

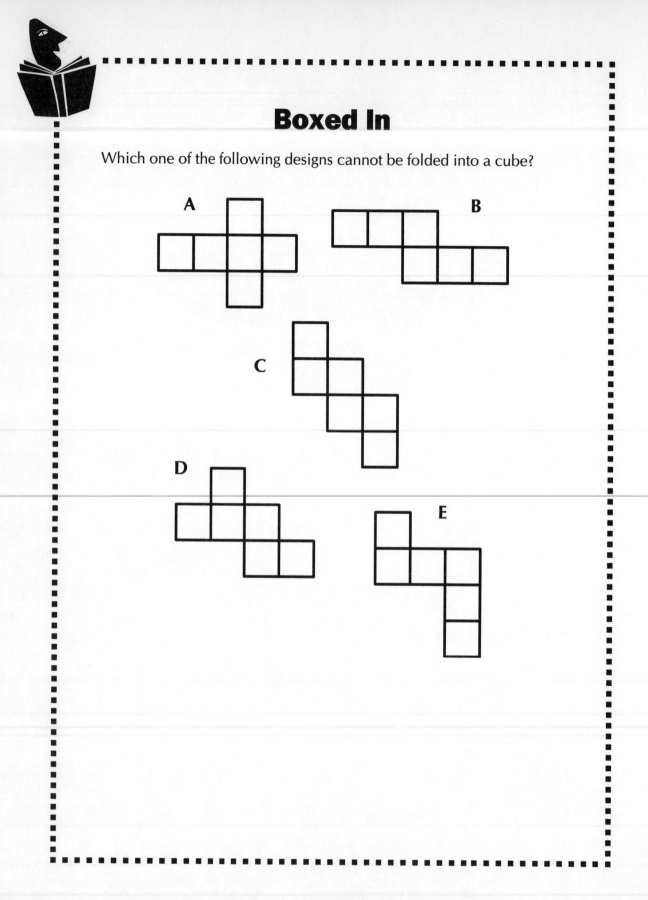

Faces Front

Suppose you can examine this five-block shape (although hidden, the fifth block is present in the middle of the shape) from any angle. How many different cube faces can you count?

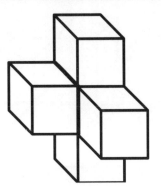

Suppose that hidden block (the fifth one) is evaporated. How many cube faces would now be exposed?

Now examine this nine-block shape from any angle. How many different cube faces can you count?

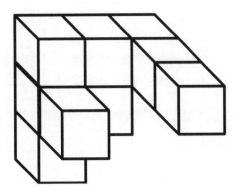

Impossible Profile

Even though you can't see the entire block structure below, you can make accurate statements about its appearance. If viewed from all directions, which one of the four profiles is impossible?

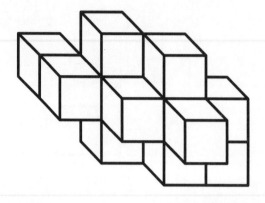

A
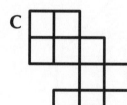

B

C
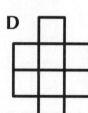

D
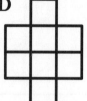

Pharoah Folds

Which of the folding patterns below will produce a shape unlike the others?

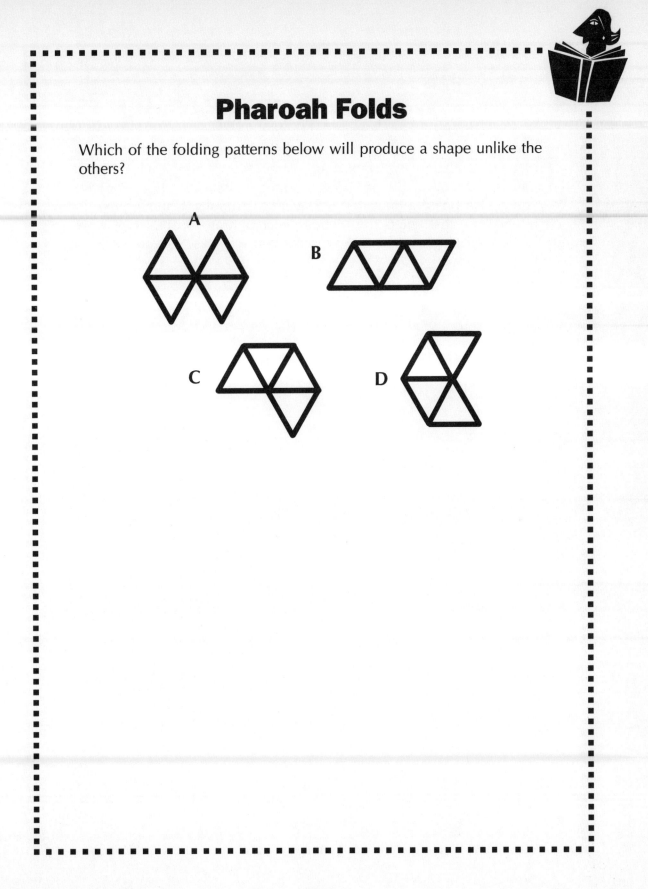

Brain Training

There are two parallel railroad tracks that connect the cities of Metropolis and Gotham City. Every hour, a train leaves from each city and travels to the other. The trip takes 3 hours in either direction. Suppose you are on board a train that is leaving Metropolis. Counting the inbound train that enters the Metropolis station as you pull out, what is the total number of inbound trains you will pass as you travel to Gotham City.

How Many Triangles?

How many equilateral triangles can you uncover in the pattern below?

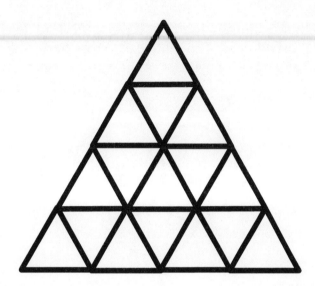

On the March

An army of neurotic ants lives in the jungle of some remote country. In their journey they've uncovered a trail formed by three overlapping circles.

    Here's the challenge: The ants have to find a route that covers every part of this odd trail. The route can't cross over itself (nor can the ants back up and retrace any steps). Can you uncover their continuous route?

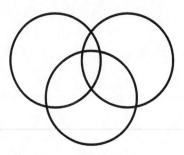

Here's route two with the same restrictions.

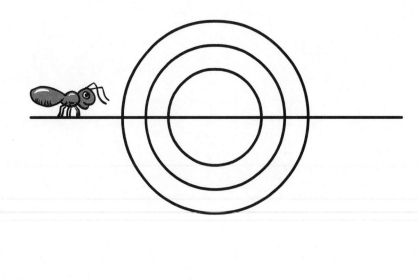

Stop and Think

How many different paths can lead you through the octagonal maze below. From start to finish, you can only move in the direction of the arrows.

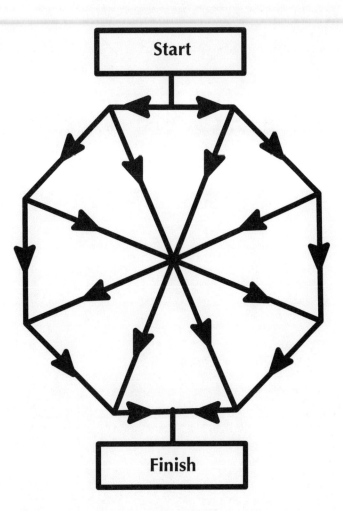

Hint: There is a way to do this puzzle without tracing out each path. Can you uncover the strategy?

Circular Code

What number belongs in the blank slice below?

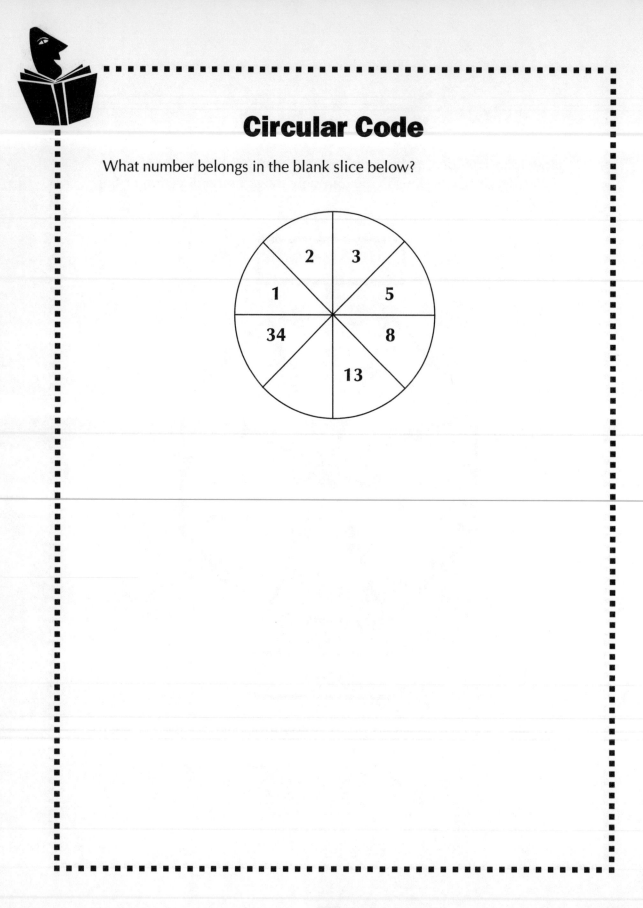

Shakes

Six people attended a gala for visual thinkers. If all guests shook hands with everyone else (no pair shook hands more than once), how many handshaking events were there?

Nesting Dolls

A nesting doll collected from the planet *Infinitum* contains a limitless number of smaller dolls. Each smaller doll is exactly half the size of the larger doll that it "nests" within. Suppose the outermost doll is one foot tall. If you are to remove all of the inner dolls (assume there are an infinite number) and place them on top of each other, how tall will the stack rise?

The Whole Truth

When John P. Cubic was placed on the stand, he was questioned about his puzzle-solving capability. He assured everyone that he was skilled in puzzeology.

To prove this, he displayed a cardboard square with an off-center hole. "By cutting this cardboard into two and only two pieces (and re-arranging those pieces), I can move the hole into the center of this square." Although the jury was out, the lie detector supported his claim.

Can you figure out his cutting pattern?

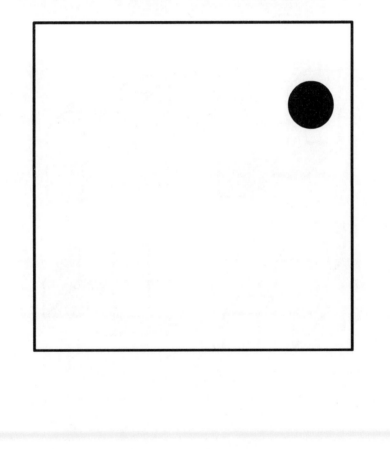

Block Heads

Which pattern of blocks is unlike the others?

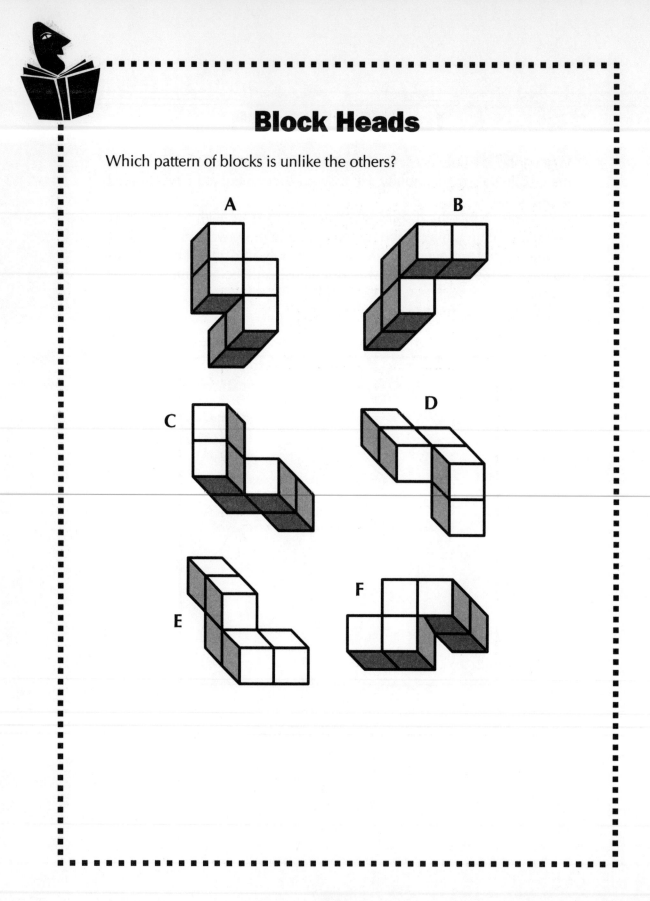

A

B

C

D

E

F

Fill 'er Up

Can you fill out the grid below using the following clues?

   a) B is in the same column as E and H.
   b) F is to the left of B and directly above D.
   c) G is to the right of E and directly above I.
   d) D is directly left of H and in the same column as A.

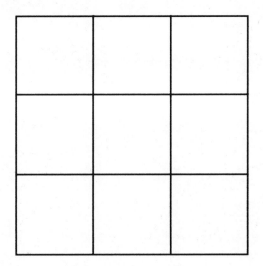

The Jig's Up

A jigsaw puzzle contains fifty pieces. If joining any two pieces (or groups of pieces) is considered one move, what is the fewest number of moves required to join all fifty pieces?

This Wheel's On Fire

Examine the two sets of wheels below. The shaft that connects both sets of wheels is made of solid steel. In the top set, the shaft is attached at the same distance above each of the wheels. In the lower pair, the shaft is attached more towards the edge of the larger wheel.

If the small wheel spins in a clockwise direction, what will happen to the larger wheel? Will the motion of the larger wheel be different in the lower pair? If so, how?

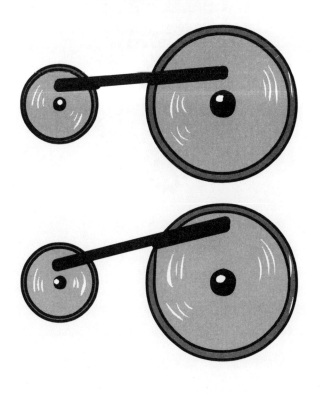

Square Gears

Suppose you were able to turn the top square gear. How much of a turn (if any) would the lower square gear make?

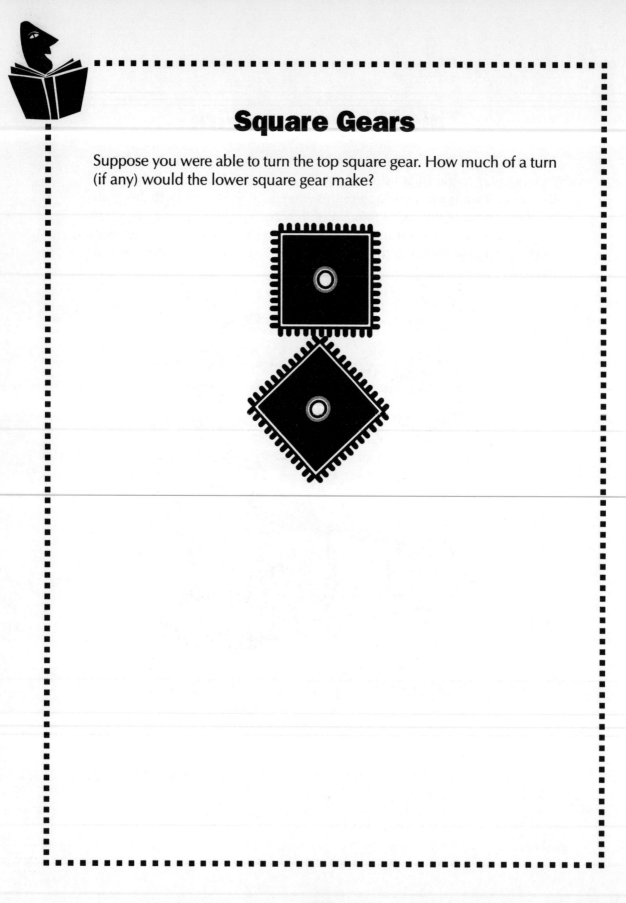

Going to Pieces

The below puzzle is entitled "White Cat on a Snowy Day in the Arctic." Suppose you have to completely color each piece so that no two adjoining pieces are the same color.

What is the minimum number of colors you need to distinguish each piece?

Toothpick Tricks

Arrange twenty-four toothpicks in the pattern below. Can you remove eight picks from this pattern so that only two squares are formed by the remaining picks?

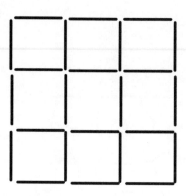

Arrange sixteen toothpicks in the pattern below. Can you *move* (don't remove) three toothpicks so that four squares of the same size are produced?

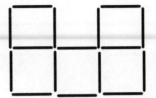

Build the house below using eleven toothpicks. Can you change the position of one toothpick to make the house face in the other direction?

Finally, arrange six toothpicks to make eight different triangles. *Hint:* The triangles will be of two different sizes.

Puzzling Pages

A blast of wind has separated the pages of a local newspaper. From the page numbers shown below, can you determine how many pages were in the complete newspaper?

Controversial Cube

Which two cubes below can be constructed by folding this pattern? Let's assume that the pattern is the "outside" of the material.

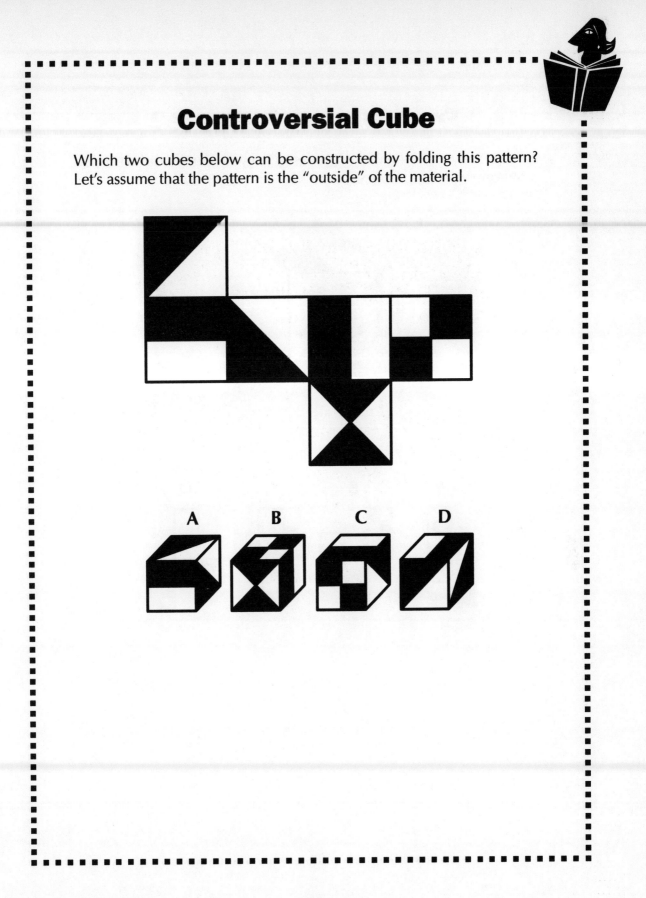

From Whence It Came?

Now let's reverse the thinking process. Can you identify the outer pattern from which the cube was folded?

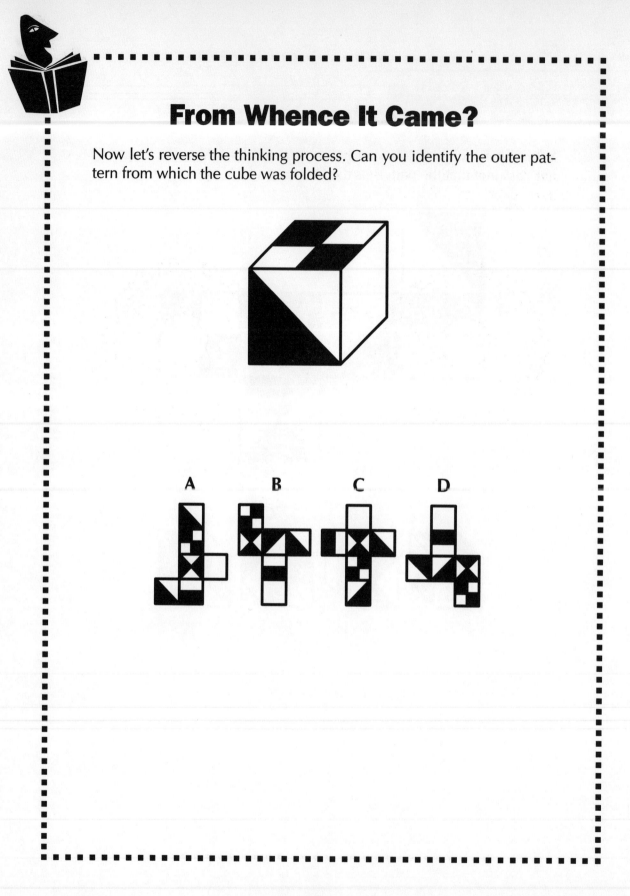

A   B   C   D

Sink Your Teeth

Both cog A and cog D have sixty teeth. Cog B has thirty teeth. Cog C has ten teeth. Suppose cog B makes twenty complete turns every minute. Which will spin faster, cog A or cog D?

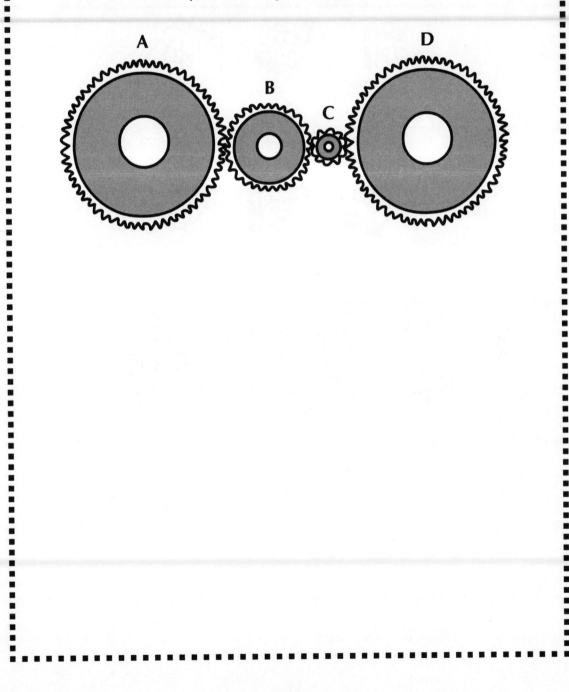

Hands-On/Minds-Off

Examine each of these hands carefully. Then decide which one of the nine is unlike all the others?

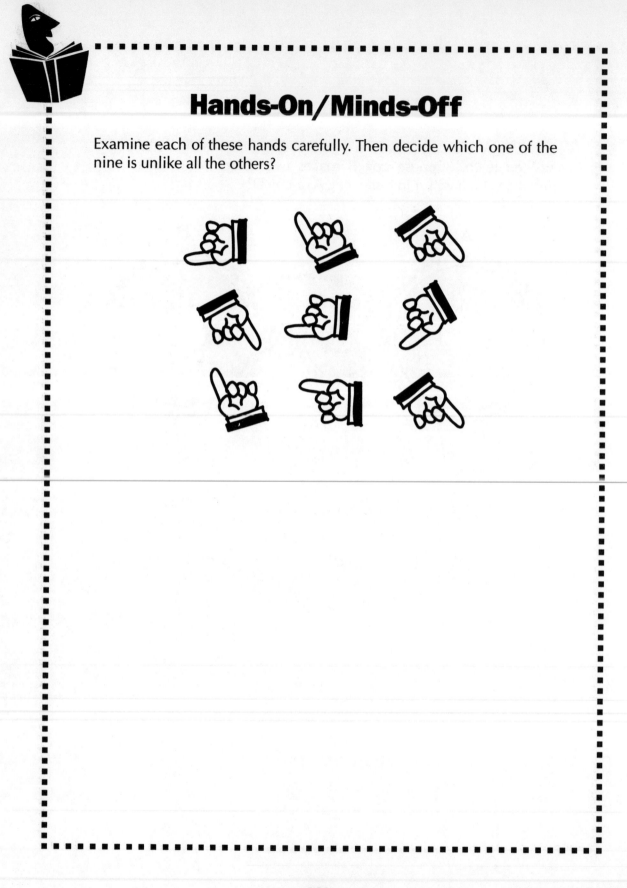

Going In Circles?

Are the belts and wheels arranged so that they will spin freely as this mouse races up the treadmill?

Spotty Answers

Can you draw an equilateral triangle so that the three dots below are positioned on different sides of the triangle?

Let's add a side to the challenge. Can you draw a square so that each of the four dots below are positioned on different sides of the square?

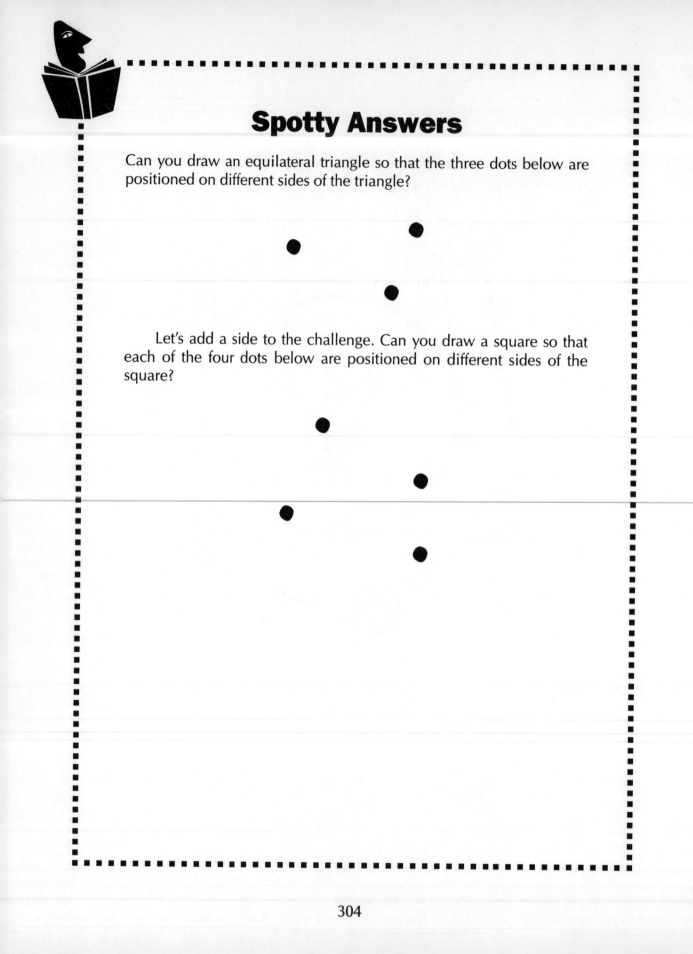

More Spots

Using only six straight lines, connect all of the sixteen dots shown below.

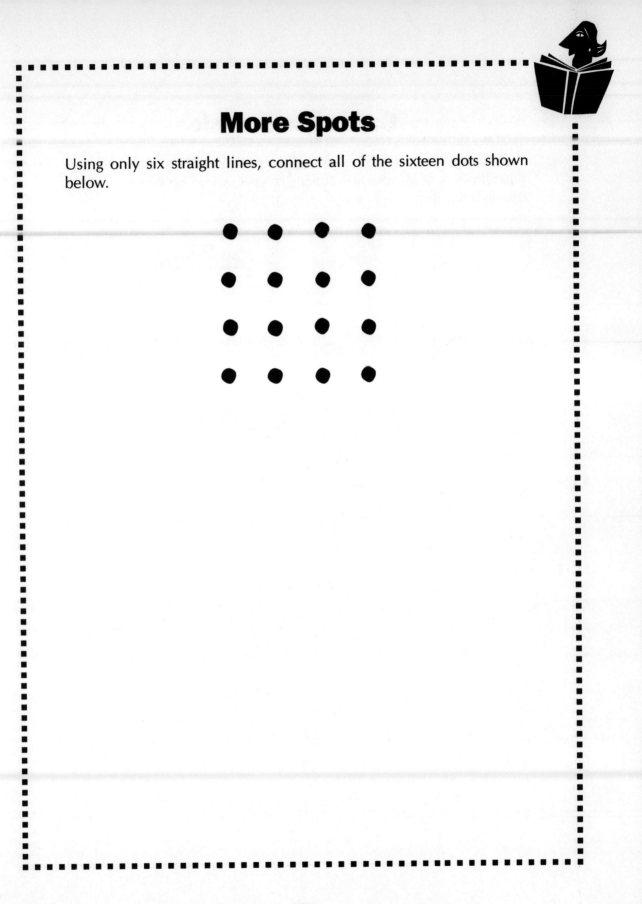

Caffeine Break

The owners of a local coffee store ordered two different sizes of coffee pots. If pot A holds about 8 ounces of java, about how many ounces does pot B hold?

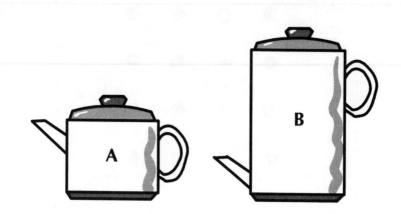

Sector Sever

Four alien civilizations are dividing up the universe. They encounter a sector of space that has this unique arrangement of planets. If all four civilizations are to get identical sectors of space (each containing three different planets), show how this region should be divided.

More of the Great Divide

The star map below gives the location of eleven stars. Can you give each star its own space by dividing the square with only five straight lines? The spaces don't have to be equal.

Let the Games Begin

When those aliens aren't dividing up the universe, they're engaging in competitive sports. So far, their favorite game is tug-of-war. During the competitions, there were three ties, which are illustrated below. From this information, can you determine which of the choices can balance the unfinished match?

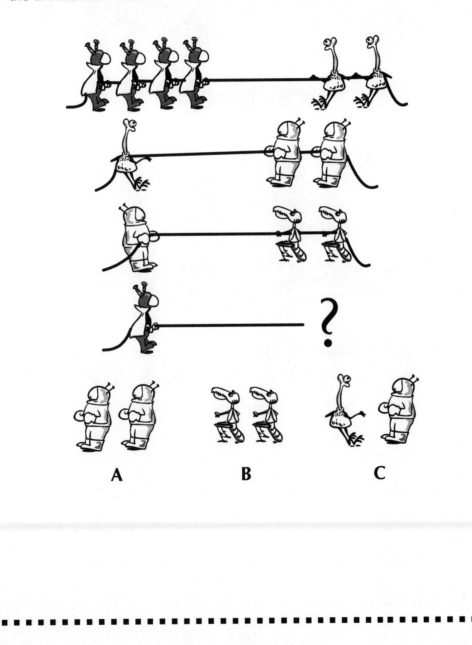

A   B   C

Sneaky

Suppose you are able to crawl inside this sneaker that belongs to one of those alien athletes. Assuming that the laces always cross, what would the inner crisscrossed view look like?

Foiling Folds

Suppose a square sheet of paper is folded and creased. Then a single snip of the scissors removes a corner of the fold as shown in the last step below. If the pattern is then unfolded, which square will it now resemble?

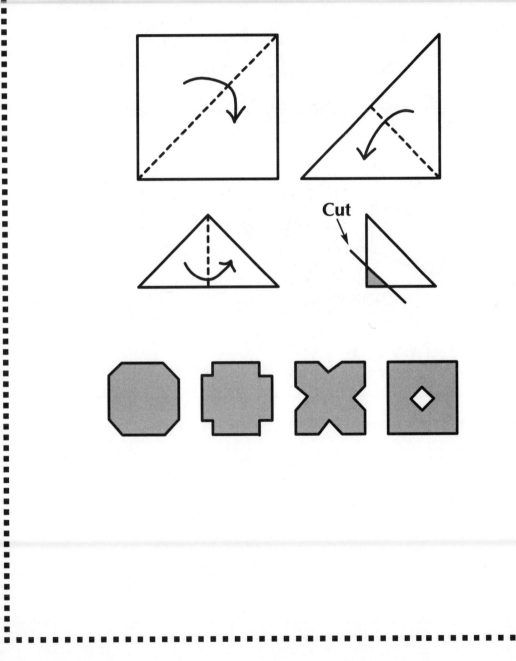

Spiral Bound

An astronomer photographs two side-by-side spiral galaxies. When she examines her files, however, she uncovers that one of the photos is of a different galaxy pair. Examine the six images below. One pair of spirals is unlike the others. Can you identify the different image?

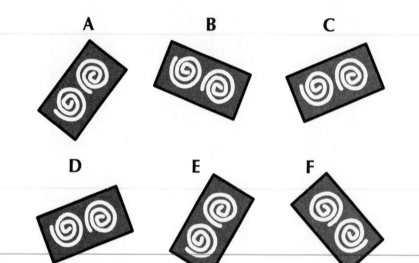

A   B   C

D   E   F

Imagining Digits

In the numbers 1 through 100, which digit appears the most? While you're at it, in that same set of numbers, which digit appears the least?

Roll With It

If you rolled this pattern into a cylinder, which one of the choices below will it look like?

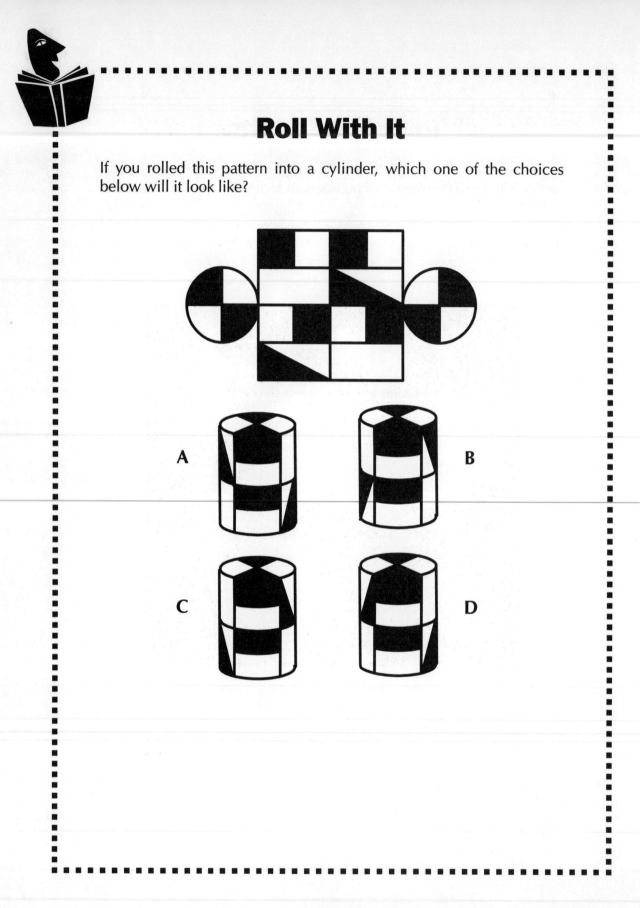

A

B

C

D

Out of This World Construction

Orbiting above the earth are the four cubic sections of a soon-to-be constructed space station. Astronauts will assemble the four separate cubes into a four-cube station. The only problem is that the astronauts left the construction plans back on Earth. It's your job to determine how many different four-cube arrangements are possible. (The cubes can only be joined squarely and face-to-face.)

Into the Pool?

Seven pool balls are placed in a pattern shown below. Can you re-arrange the balls so that the sum of any three-ball line is equal to twelve?

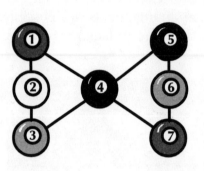

Sure Shot

Suppose the billiard ball strikes the bumper at the point identified by the arrow. If the ball has the energy to keep rolling, which pocket will it eventually sink into?

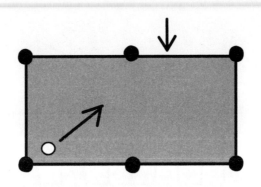

Coaster Cut

Alas, the party is over and the amusement park is closed. The roller coaster ride has been sold. All that is left is this one section of track and frame. In order to be moved, the pattern must be divided into two identical parts. Can you do it?

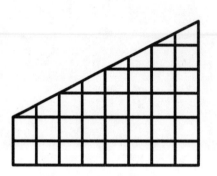

Sizing Up Squares

How many different sizes of square can be made by connecting the dots that form this grid? And while you are at it, what is the total number of squares that can be created by connecting the pattern dots?

The Circle Game

Can you uncover the pattern in the following figure? If so, use what you've discovered to identify the number that should be placed in the center of the figure.

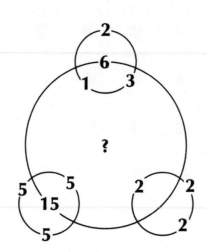

What's Next?

Complete this sequence.

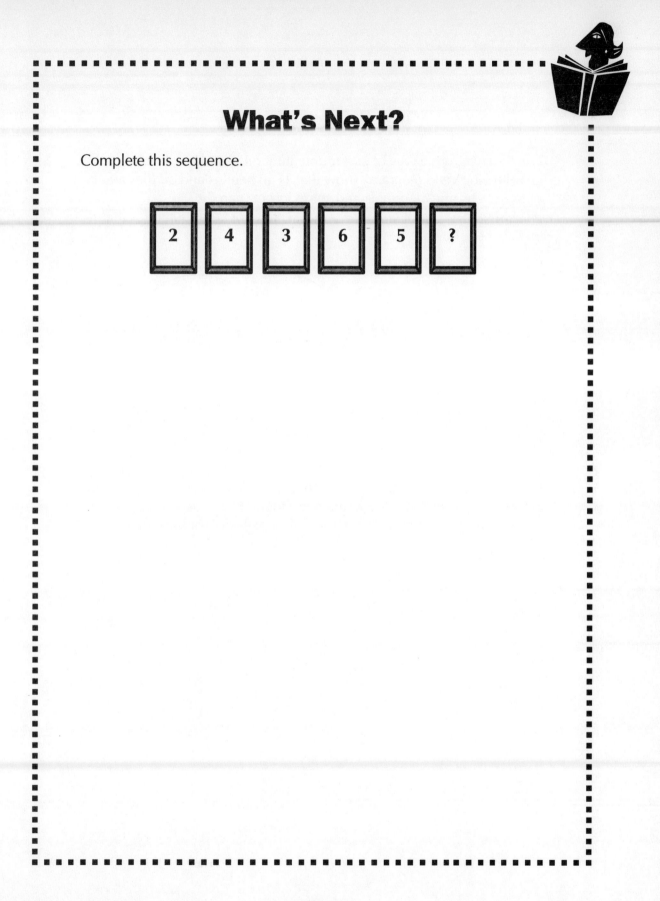

Very Well Venn

A Venn diagram is a way of communicating relationships. For example, the following Venn diagrams show that 1) all beetles and all flies are insects and 2) some mammals and some insects can fly.

Using this type of visual scheme, sketch out Venn diagrams that illustrate the following:

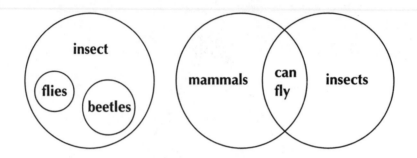

1. All ice creams are dairy products and all dairy products are food.
2. Some rockets use liquid fuel, some rockets use solid fuel, and the space shuttle uses both liquid and solid fuel.
3. All whales and all dogs have hair. All snakes do not have hair.

Rack 'Em . . . Again, Again, and Again

The pool balls below are positioned in a six-ball rack. If you add the values of any three-ball edge, you'll come up with ten. Can you re-arrange the balls within this rack to produce three other patterns that also produce equal-sum sides?

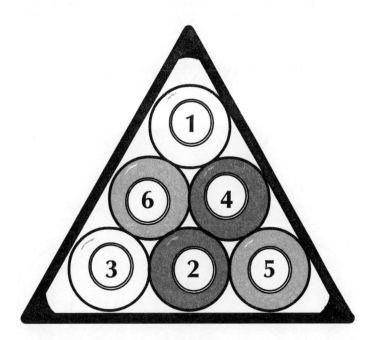

Dial Dilemma

The instruments in a cockpit are positioned so that a pilot can quickly glance at the indicators and know instantly if there is a problem. In the panel below, one dial does not fit the pattern. Can you locate it quickly?

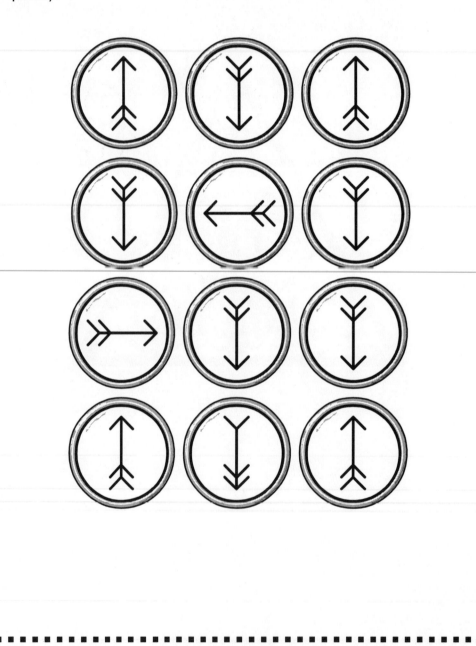

Troubling Tree

Can you uncover the pattern in this "tree" and use it to solve for the missing number?

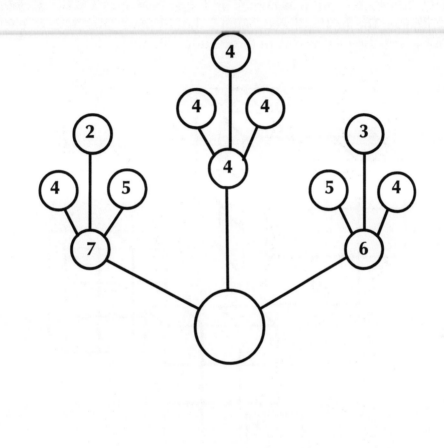

Three-Colored Cube

The cube below has been cut into twenty-seven smaller cubes. These cubes can viewed as three nine-cube slices. So far, so good? Great. Here's where the hard part comes in. Using one of three colors, color each cube. The final colored pattern should have one cube of each color in any three-cube row or three-cube column.

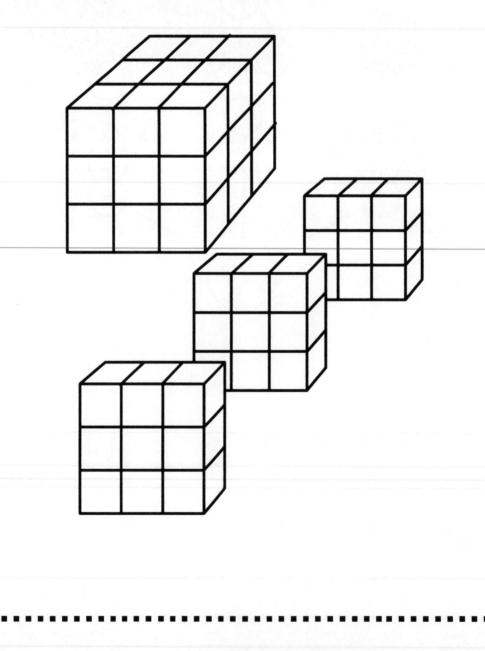

Trying Triangles

Copy these six patterns onto a sheet of heavy-stock paper. Use a pair of scissors to carefully cut them out. Arrange the shapes into one equal-sided triangle.

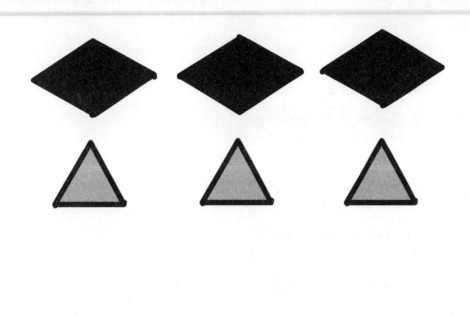

Here, Spot

Suppose you could fill in any of the circles of this pattern. How many different and distinguishable patterns could you make?

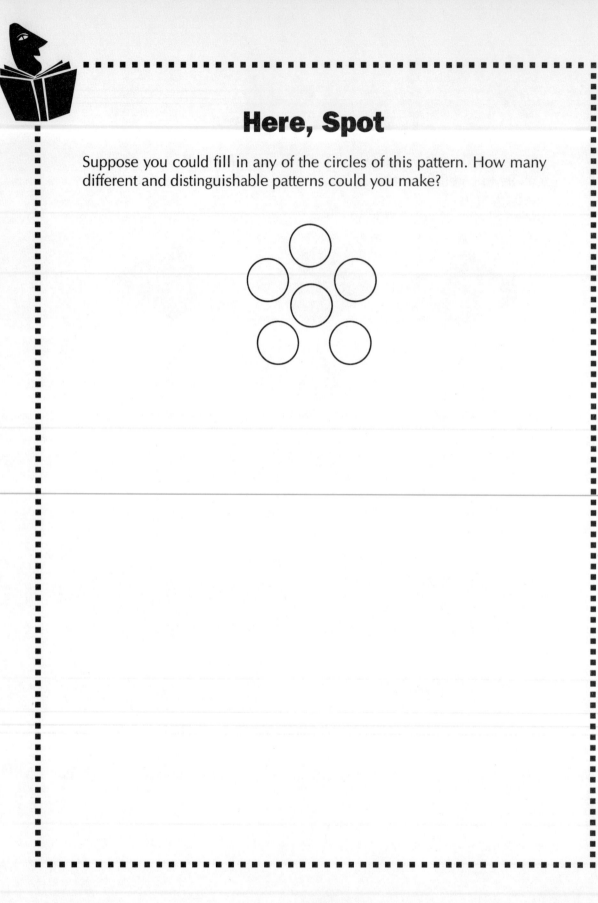

Chalk One Up

A large chalk stick has a diameter of an inch. The chalk is packed in a box whose inner space measures 5" × 4". Within this space, twenty pieces of chalk fit snugly. If the box length and width are increased as shown below, the new larger box should hold a maximum of 120 pieces of chalk. Right? Wrong. It can now hold 131 pieces of chalk.

Can you figure out how these extra eleven pieces of chalk fit?

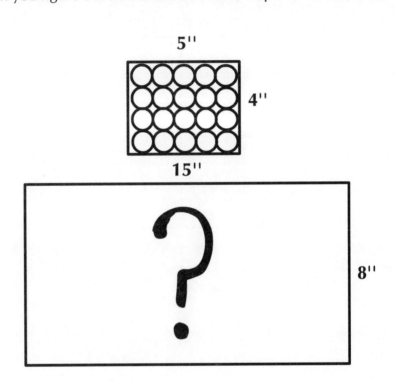

Grid-Lock

How many different ways can you divide this 4 × 4 grid into two identical parts?

Remember that all of your "dividing lines" must follow along the lines that are all ready in place. Do not count as different ones those that are simply rotations or reflections of others.

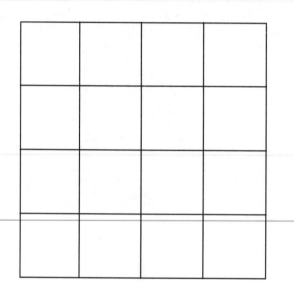

Only the Shadow Knows

Try to imagine a shape that can produce several different shadows. When illuminated from below, it casts a circular shadow. When illuminated from the north, it casts a rectangular shadow. When illuminated from the east, it casts a triangular shadow.

What is the shape of the actual object?

Lucky Eleven?

By connecting different dot sets, you should be able to form eleven different shapes of triangles. Good luck!

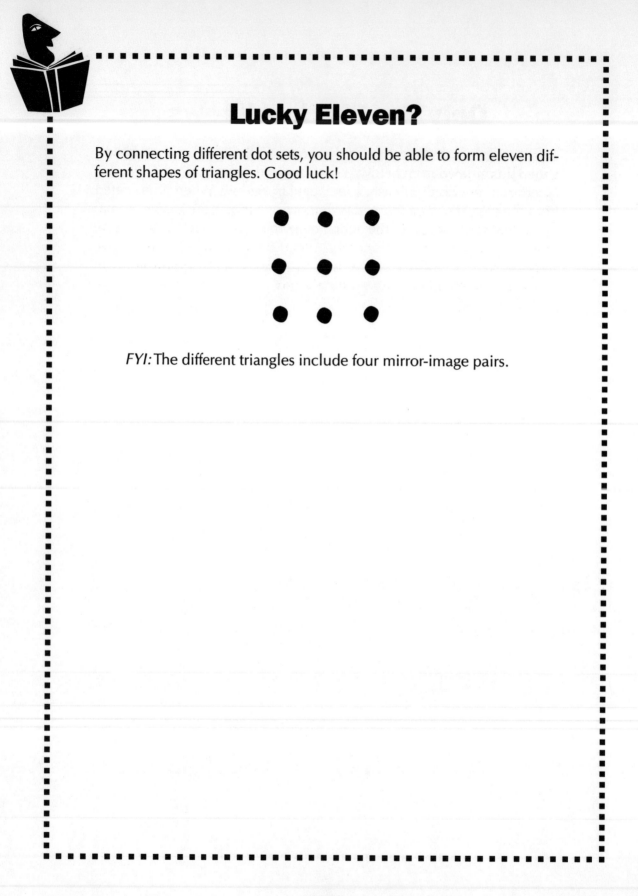

FYI: The different triangles include four mirror-image pairs.

Station Spread

Scientists often use visual models to help understand and communicate ideas. Although the following problem is on a global scale, perhaps you can visualize a desktop version of the situation?

Scientists are designing a network of earthquake-monitoring stations. The stations can be built on any surface, but must be located at equal distances from one another. What is the maximum number of stations that can be placed on the Earth and remain equidistant? Oh yes, and where will the stations be placed?

ANSWERS

Amaze in String

It will come free of the pipe. To visualize this action, start at the pipe. From there, trace the pipe's path out from the center. After a few turns, the pipe exits freely at the opening on the right side of the maze.

Block Heads

E.

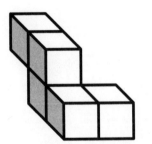

Boxed In

E cannot be folded into a cube.

Brain Training

Six. At every half hour of the journey, you'll pass an incoming train. If you count the inbound train in the Metropolis station and don't count the inbound train in the Gotham City station, you'll pass six trains.

Broken Record

b) spiral in towards the center spindle (its normal motion). Both sides of the record have an identical spiral. Therefore, if the grooves align, the needle will follow its normal motion towards the center spindle.

Caffeine Break

4 ounces (about half of pot A). The amount of coffee that can be kept within each pot is determined by the height of the spout opening. The coffee level cannot rise above that spout opening since any extra coffee would spill out from the spout.

Circular Code

21. As you move clockwise around the circle, the number on each section is equal to the sum of the two previous sections.

Coaster Cut

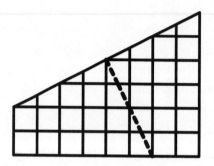

Code Caper

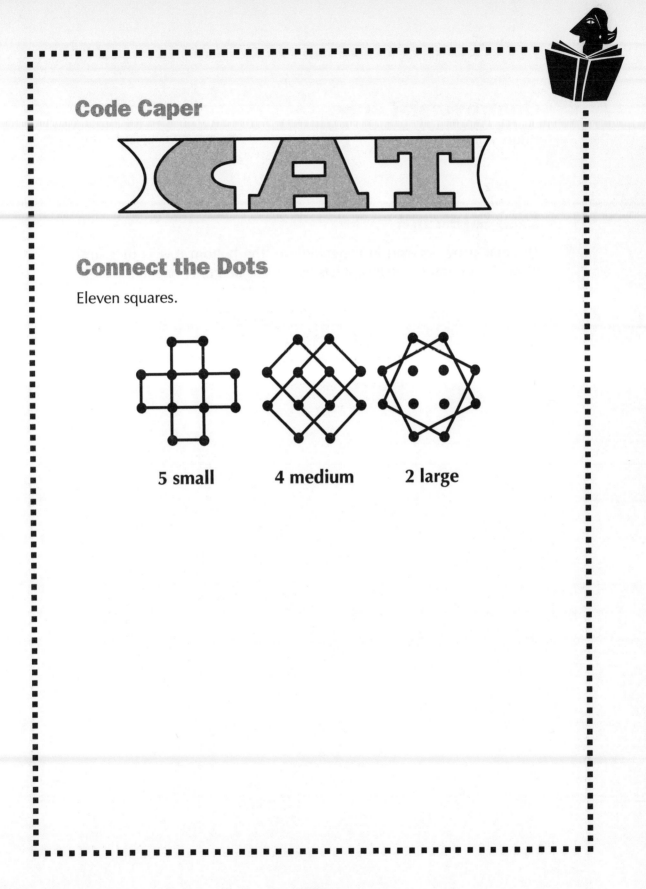

Connect the Dots

Eleven squares.

5 small   **4 medium**   **2 large**

Controversial Cube

Cubes A and D.

Dial Dilemma

The dial arrow located in the middle of the bottom row is most un-usual. In contrast to the rest, it has two heads and only one tail.

Faces Front

Part I: Twenty-two sides.
Part II: Thirty-six sides.

Fill 'er Up

A	E	G
F	B	I
D	H	C

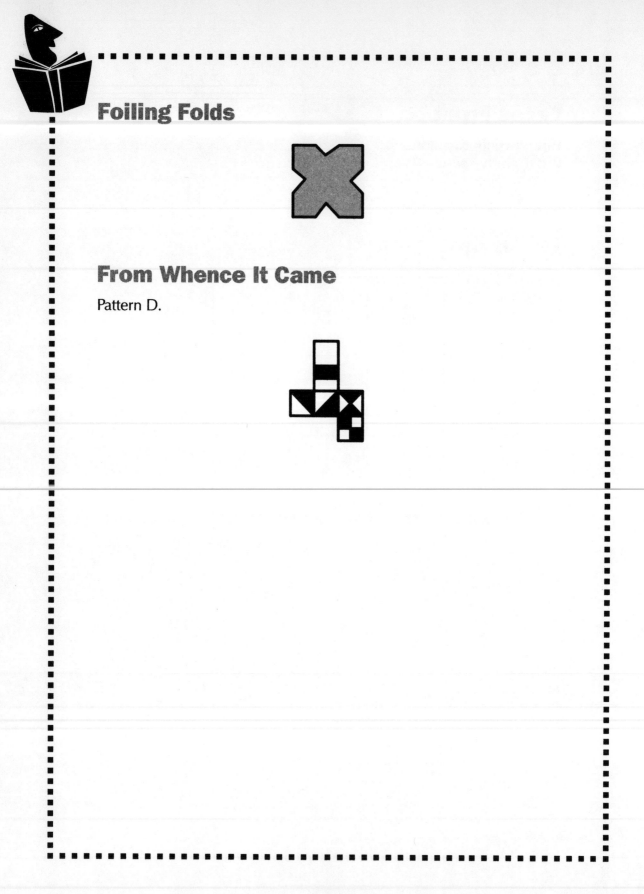

Foiling Folds

From Whence It Came

Pattern D.

Going in Circles?

No, the belts are arranged in a pattern that doesn't allow them to move.

Going to Pieces

Four colors. It doesn't matter how many common borders there are. The maximum number of colors needed to distinguish any number of adjoining pieces will always be four.

Hands-On/Minds-Off

The bottom-row center hand is unlike the others. It alone is a right hand.

Hidden in Plane Site

The fifteen squares are:
one 4 × 4 square;
two 3 × 3 squares;
four 2 × 2 squares;
eight 1 × 1 square.

Imagining Digits

The digit 1 appears 21 times. The digit 0 appears only 11 times.

Impossible Profile

C.

**cube
not
shown**

345

Grid-Lock

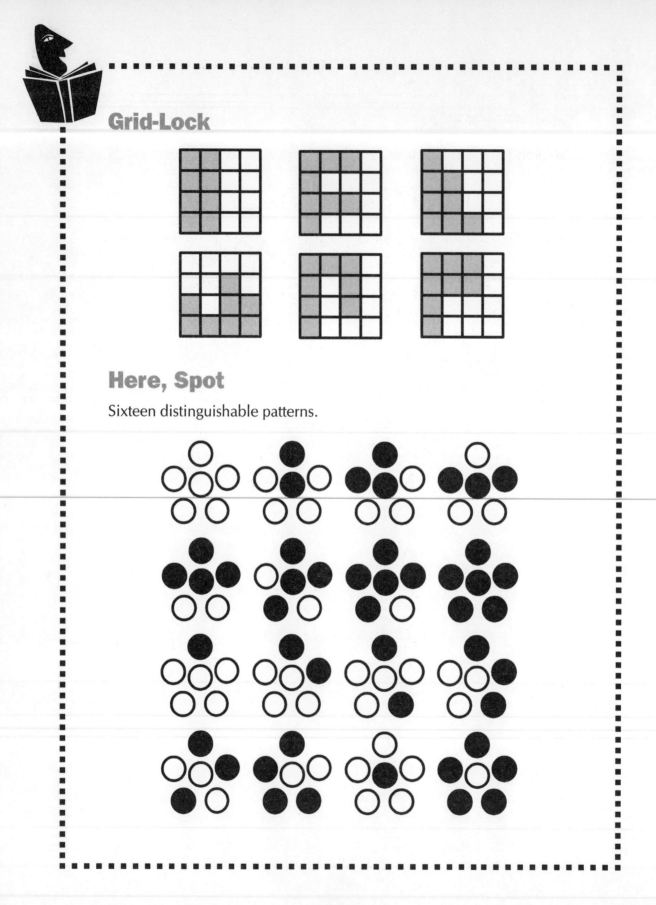

Here, Spot

Sixteen distinguishable patterns.

Into the Pool

Two solutions are shown.

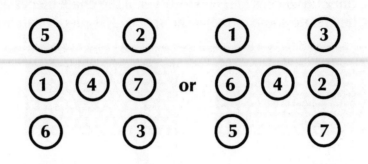

Let the Games Begin

B. Here's why:

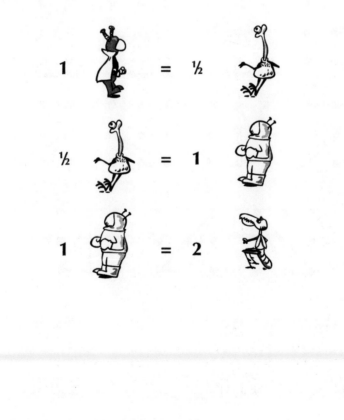

Chalk One Up

It all depends upon how you pack the chalk. In straight rows and columns, only 120 pieces can fit. However, if the chalk pieces are staggered so they fill up some of the waste space, 131 pieces can fit.

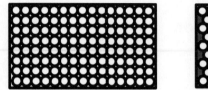 

Lucky Eleven

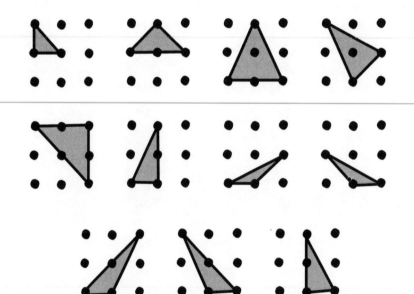

Troubling Tree

9. The numbers are obtained by adding together the values of the two circles that are attached by diagonal lines. Then the value within the circle directly atop is subtracted from this sum. In the final grouping, it's 7 + 6 – 9, or 9.

Link Latch

Just open the bottom link. The top two links are not attached to each other.

Mirror Madness

A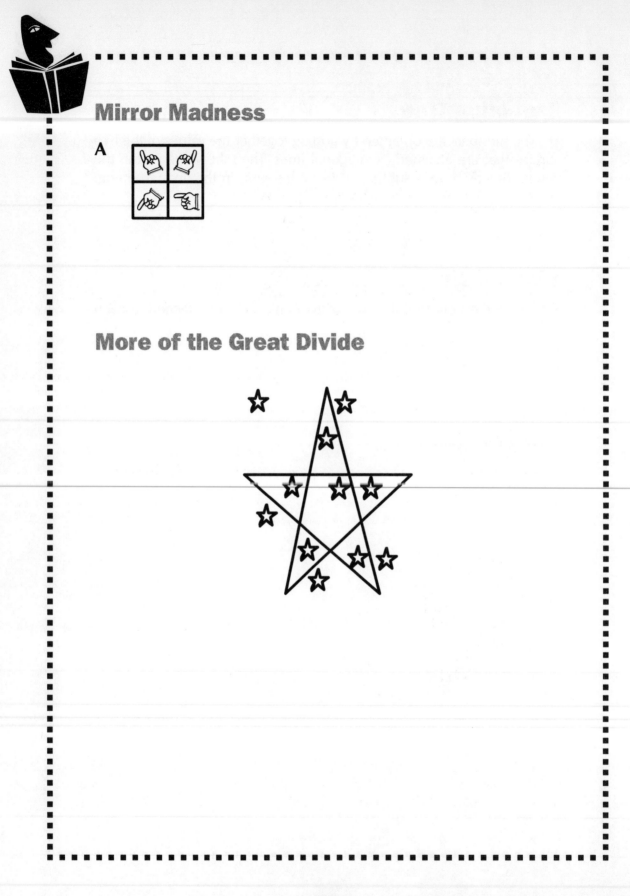

More of the Great Divide

More Spots

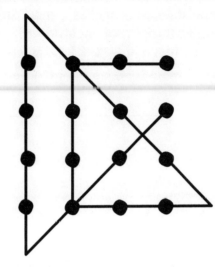

Naughty Notes

G is a mirror image of the other note pairs. All other pairs can be made by rotating another pair.

G

Nesting Dolls

The final height of the stack approaches 2 feet. Although there are an infinite number of dolls, the size of each doll diminishes. Mathematically that works out to 1 ft. + ½ ft. + ¼ ft. + ⅛ ft. + ⅟₁₆ ft. + ⅟₃₂ ft. . . .

On the March

Part I   **Part II**

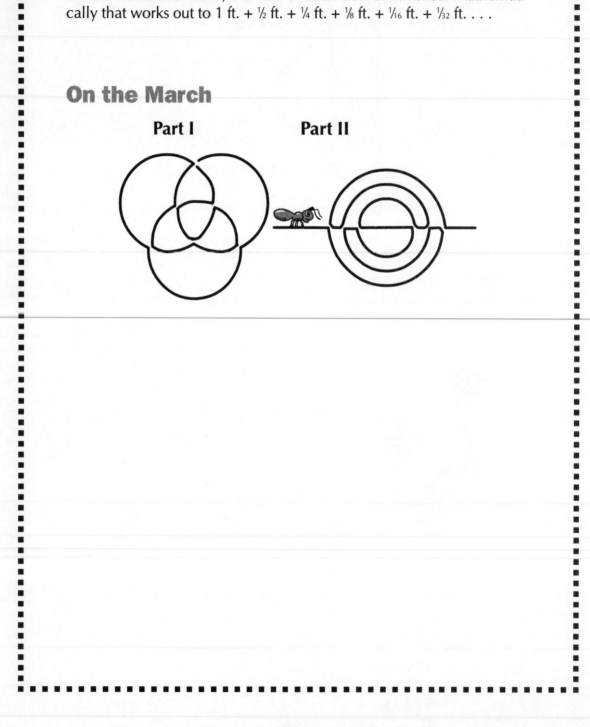

Out of This World Construction

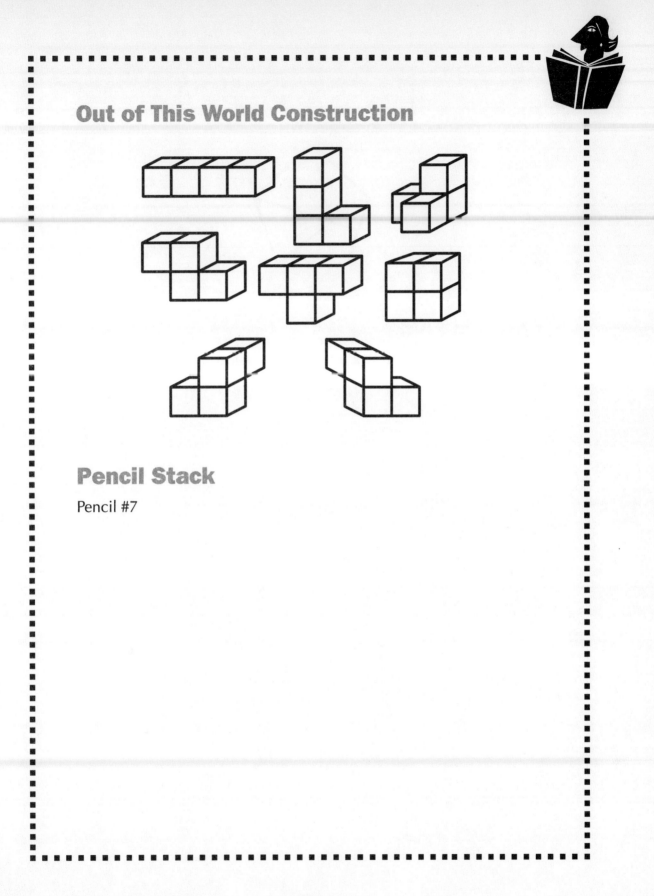

Pencil Stack

Pencil #7

Pentagon Pieces

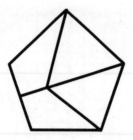

Pharoah Folds

B is the only pattern that will produce a four-sided triangular pyramid.

Pi Pieces

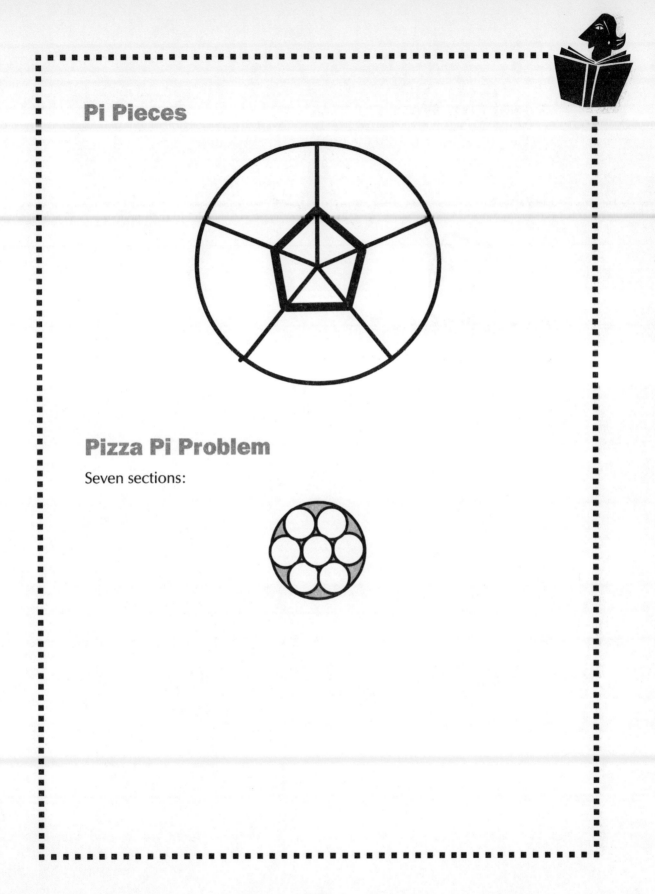

Pizza Pi Problem

Seven sections:

Point the Way

D. Each tile is rotated from the pervious one by ¼ turn.

Prefab 4

C

Trying Triangles

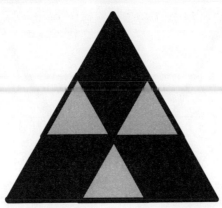

Puzzling Pages

56 pages. Here's how the numbers are arranged on each double sheet.

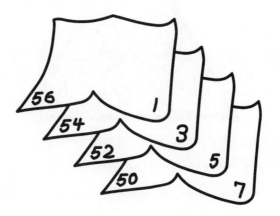

Rack Em, Again, Again, and Again

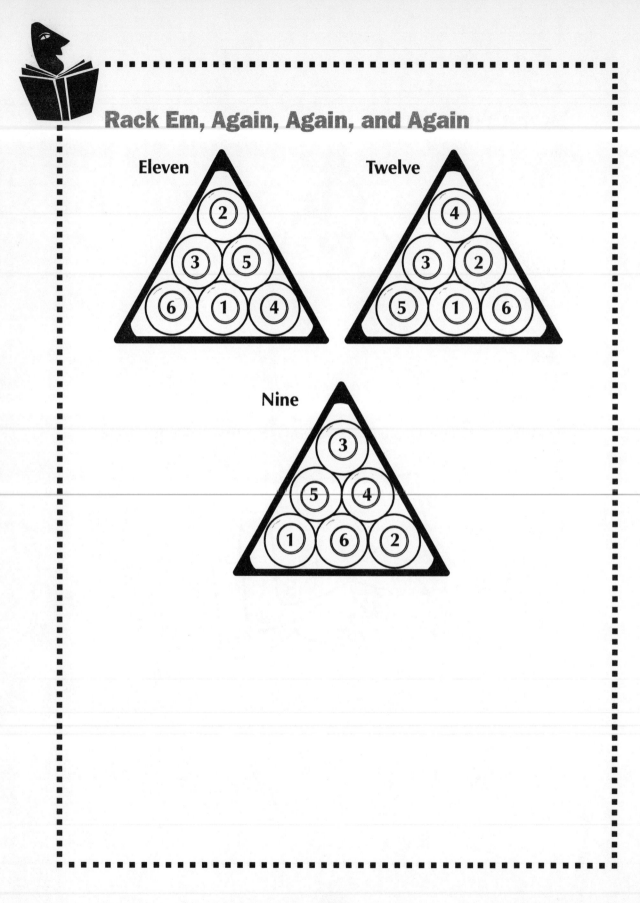

Reflecting Back

Part I

IV

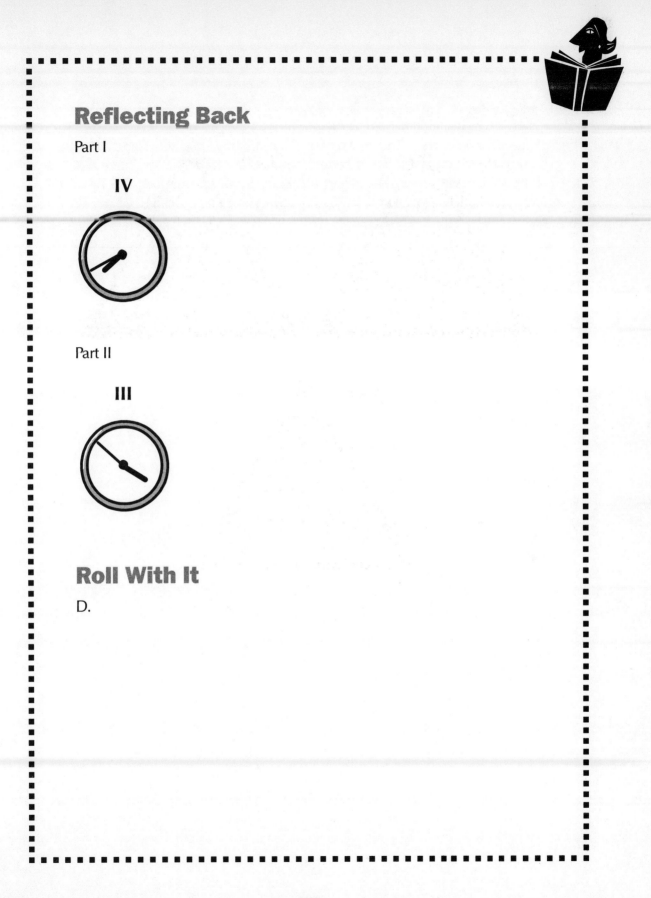

Part II

III

Roll With It

D.

Shakes

Fifteen handshakes. The first person would have shaken hands five times. The next person only needed to make four handshakes, since the handshake with one person had all ready been completed. The next person required only three, and so on. That gives us 5+4+3+2+1 = 15.

Sink Your Teeth

Since they have the same number of teeth, they will spin at the same speed. Cog C does not affect the rate of teeth passage; it only transfers the passage of teeth from cog B to cog D.

SECTOR SEVER

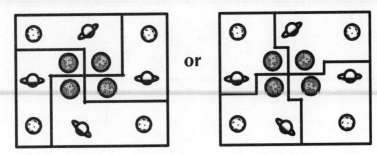

or

SIZING UP SQUARES

Five sizes:

Twenty squares.

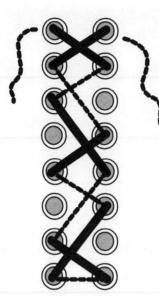

Spacing Out

No. To best visualize her path, let's undo the cube into its component flattened faces. From this diagram, you can see that the shortest distance between two points is a straight line. That line does not coincide with her planned path (shown as a dotted line).

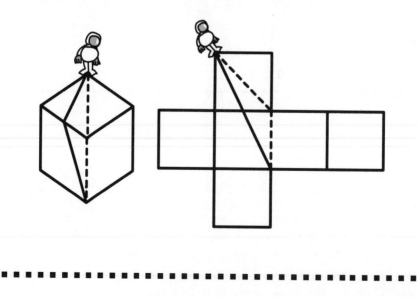

Spiral Bound

Block F. All five other blocks are identical. Block F is a mirror image of these blocks.

Spotty Answers

Part I

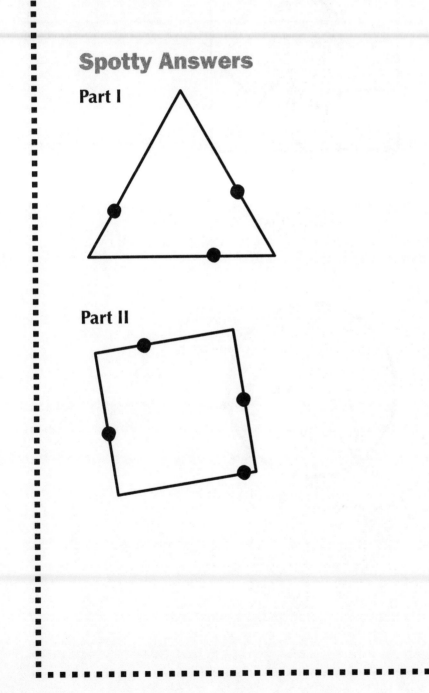

Part II

Square Deal

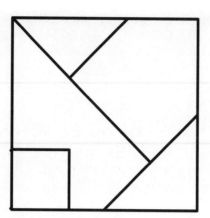

Station Spread

Four stations. Each station is placed at the corner of a four-sided pyramid (tetrahedron) that is inscribed within the planet.

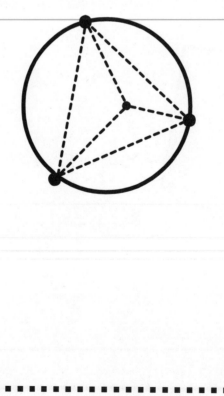

Square Gears

The bottom gear would continue to spin as if both gears were circular.

Stop and Think

Eighteen, but you don't have to trace out each one. The easiest way to solve this puzzle is to start at the beginning and determine the number of paths that can get you to an intersection. The number of paths to each successive intersection is equal to the sum of the paths that are "attached" to it.

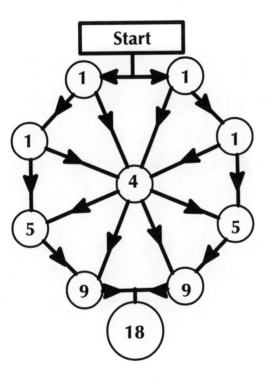

Superimposing Position

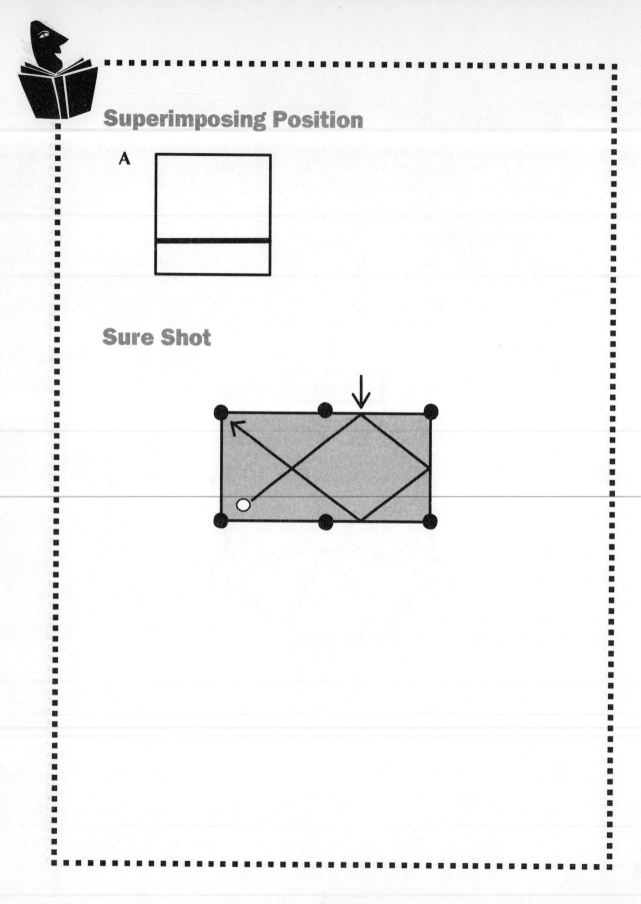

A

Sure Shot

Only the Shadow Knows

It is a cylinder that has been cut into a wedge. Two slices that extend from the upper diameter to opposite sides of the bottom have been removed to form this shape.

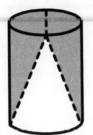

The Circle Game

27. The number at the center of any circle is equal to the sum of the number located on its outline.

The Jig's Up

Forty-nine moves. The sequence and strategy in which the pieces are assembled will not affect the number of moves. Fifty pieces require forty-nine independent joining "events".

The Whole Truth

Cut out an L-shaped section and rotate it to the opposite corner of the piece with the hole.

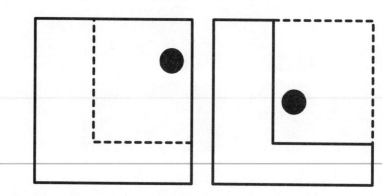

This Side Up

The extra figure is "formed" within the center of this pattern.

Toothpick Tricks

Part I

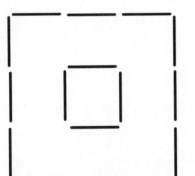

Part II

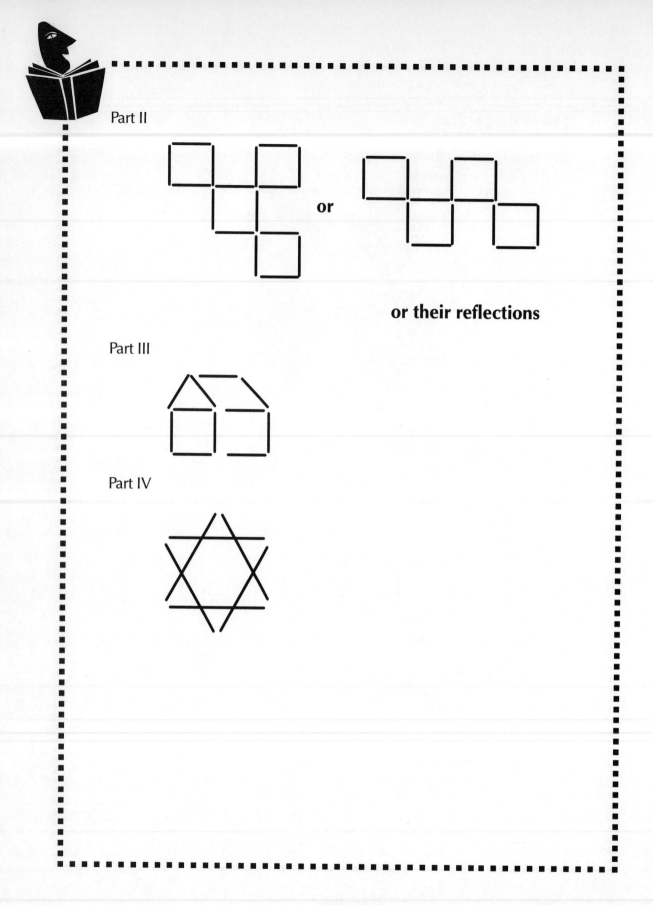

or

or their reflections

Part III

Part IV

How Many Triangles?

27 triangles: 16 one-cell triangles, 7 four-cell triangles, 3 nine-cell triangles, and 1 sixteen-cell triangle.

Tying the Knot

A knot *will* form in the spaghetti.

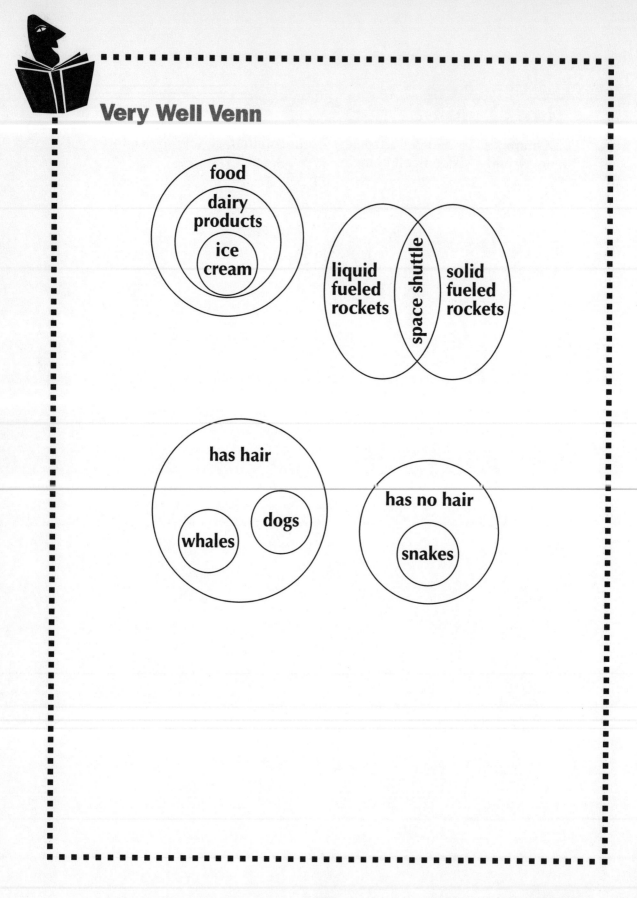

Three-Colored Cube

This Wheel's On Fire

In the top set, the large wheel will spin the exact same way as the smaller wheel. In the bottom set, the top wheel will first move clockwise. Then, before completing a rotation, it will reverse direction.

What's Next?

10. The sequence is formed by first doubling a number and then subtracting one from the product.

What Sign Are You?

$$5 \; \boxed{\times} \; 2 \; \boxed{-} \; 3 \; \boxed{+} \; 5 \; \boxed{\div} \; 4 = 3$$

Wrap It Up

c.

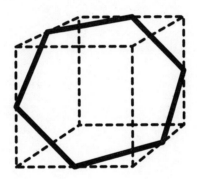

Cut the Cube

The cut must bisect the cube in half as shown below. The exposed inner surface is flat and has the shape of a hexagon.

INDEX
Answers appear on pages in *italics.*